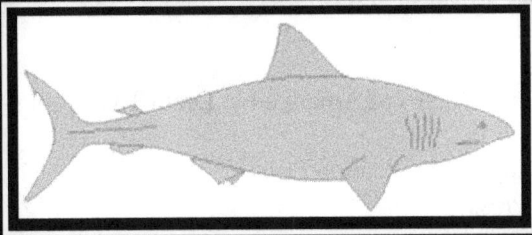

GREAT WHITE SHARKS
OF THE
CAROLINAS & GEORGIA

By
John Hairr

Dram Tree
Books

First Edition 2009
Published in the United States of America by Dram Tree Books.

Publisher's Cataloging-in-Publication Data
(Provided by DRT Press)

Publisher's Cataloging-in-Publication data

Hairr, John.
   Shark! Great white sharks of the Carolinas & Georgia / by John Hairr.
   p. cm.
   Includes bibliographical references and index.
   ISBN 978-0-9814603-8-3
1. Sharks. 2. White shark. 3. Sharks—North Carolina. 4. Sharks—South Carolina. 5. Sharks—Georgia. 6. Sharks—Atlantic Ocean. I. Shark! Great white sharks of the Carolinas and Georgia. II. Title.

QL795.S46°H34 2009
597.3—dc22

10 9 8 7 6 5 4 3 21

Dram Tree Books
P.O. Box 7183
Wilmington, N.C. 28406
(910) 538-4076
www.dramtreebooks.com
Potential authors: visit our website or email us for submission guidelines

Volume discounts available.
Call or e-mail for terms.

FOR SHELBY

CONTENTS

ACKNOWLEDGEMENTS

G reat white sharks captivate the minds of shark enthusiasts around the world. Images of these huge fish stalking divers in an iron cage or blasting out of the water in quest of a seal decoy towed behind a boat fill books, magazines, websites and television documentaries. But nearly all these encounters are from faraway places such as Australia, South Africa or California. The presence of these remarkable fish have been thoroughly chronicled from other shores but their presence in the waters off the southeastern United States, from Chesapeake Bay to the Gulf of Mexico, is often overlooked in the shark literature and documentaries, where the sighting or landing of a white shark is often viewed as an aberration. Thus, this book began as an inquiry into the question of whether great white sharks are a normal part of the natural ecosystem of the coastal region of the southeastern United States, or whether their presence here along our shores is just an anomaly.

To accomplish this, it was necessary to delve into the historical record to find accounts of white shark encounters from the past, as well as to interview individuals from modern times who have direct knowledge of white sharks in recent years. The results of my efforts can be found in the pages of this book.

To gain a historical perspective of white shark encounters along our coast, it was necessary to seek out accounts from old documents such as newspapers, books, magazines, scholarly journals, and manuscripts. The reader will find a list of these at the end of this book in the bibliography.

To gain a better understanding of white shark encounters in recent years, it was necessary to interview those who have first-hand knowledge of these animals, be they marine scientists who study the various creatures that inhabit the offshore realm, recreational boaters who have reported chance encounters with white sharks, fishermen who have landed them, or anyone else who has been fortunate enough to see one of these rare sharks off our coast. I logged thousands of miles traveling to sites along the coast of the southeastern United States in order to track down people who have reported encounters with white sharks in our waters, and to learn their stories firsthand. In addition, I have spent countless hours utilizing the latest technological marvels of communication conducting interviews and listening to stories of shark encounters. All of this was done in an effort to gain a comprehensive knowledge of encounters with white sharks in these waters. I would like to take this opportunity to thank the numerous individuals who gave freely of their time to share stories of encounters with great whites off our coast. The results of many of these interviews are shared in the text.

To help put these white shark encounters in their proper perspective, I tracked down and interviewed scientists and other specialists with particular knowledge in the field of Marine Biology and Ichthyology. They were able to help me understand not only the white sharks, but also shed light on the world under the waves of which we are only now starting to explore. Without their help, this book would not have been possible, and I would like to take this opportunity to acknowledge them and thank them for their kind assistance.

In addition to recollections of his shark hunting days off the North Carolina coast, Jon Dodrill of the Florida Fish and Wildlife Commission was extremely helpful in providing background information on marine life in general, and sharks in particular; Dr. Frank Schwartz of the University of North Carolina's Institute of Marine Sciences at Morehead City was especially helpful with his advice and encouragement; Bob Roush, Bill Parker and John Woods III of the North Carolina Aquarium at Fort Fisher; Dan Palmer of *Marineland of Florida*; Henry Ansley and Leigh Youngner of the Georgia Department of Natural Resources; Dr. Jose Castro of NOAA's Southeast Fisheries Center in Miami; Dr. Dan Abel of Coastal Carolina University; Glenn Reed, former proprietor of *Shark's Tooth Cove*; Dr. Steve Ross of the University of North Carolina at Wilmington; Alexia Morgan and George Burgess of the International Shark Attack File in the Florida Museum of Natural History in Gainesville, Florida; Tim Handsel and Joe Choromanski of the Ripley's Believe It or Not® Aquarium at Myrtle Beach; Claude Bain,

Virginia Saltwater Fishing Tournament; Jim Francesconi of the North Carolina Division of Marine Fisheries; Don Hammond of the South Carolina Department of Natural Resources; Monica Zani, coordinator of right whale research for the New England Aquarium; Albert Sanders of the Charleston Museum; Dr. Wayne Starnes of the North Carolina State Museum of Natural Sciences.

Finally, I would like to express my appreciation to all the folks who shared their time, stories, photos, and other information.

INTRODUCTION

Carrying such fearsome names as "Maneater" or "the Perfect Predator," the great white shark, *Carcharodon carcharias*, is perhaps the most feared creature in the sea. These large sharks have been the subjects of awe, fascination and trepidation for generations.

When most people think of great whites in North America, they frequently conjure up images of places with cool waters such as California or New England. Great whites are often drawn to those shores because of the sea lions and seals that are resident and are a prime source of food. But great white sharks are not restricted to these cool regions. Rather, these fish are highly migratory with a circumglobal temperate ocean distribution, with some even ranging into warm tropical seas. They can be found in virtually all of the coastal regions of the United States, including the long stretch of coast from Cape Hatteras to the Florida Keys, and into the Gulf of Mexico.

Great white sharks are one of the more than 450 species of sharks swimming around in the world's oceans. Sharks are of course fish, and thus share several characteristics with other fish, such as possessing gills for breathing, living in water, and having a vertebral column. But not all fish are the same, and that is why scientists divide them into classes, orders, families, etc.. Sharks, rays, and chimaeras are a class of fish known as Chondrichthyes, as their skeletons are made up of cartilage instead of bone. Chondrichthyes are divided into two subclasses-the Holocephali and the Elasmobranchii. The former is made up of fish such as the chimaera whose cranium and upper jaw are "fused" together.

The Elasmobranchii are broken down into two suborders, the Batoidei and the Selachii. Stingrays, skates and mantas are batoids, while all species of sharks are selachians. There are eight orders of selachians that include all species of sharks. These are Hexanchiformes, Squaliformes, Pristiophoriformes, Heterodontiformes, Squatiniformes, Orectolobiformes, Carchariniformes, and Laminiformes.

Seven families of sharks make up the order Lamniformes. These sharks share such traits as having five gill openings, a long mouth that extends past the eye, an anal fin and two dorsal fins. These sharks are aplacental livebearers, which means they hatch from an egg inside the mother's uterus, and live there until they are born. Several species are known to practice a form of cannibalism by feeding on the embryos of their weaker siblings before birth.

There are five species of sharks that make up the mackerel shark family Lamnidae, which includes the great white. The other lamnids include shortfin and longfin mako sharks, the porbeagle shark, and the salmon shark.

Great white sharks have two dorsal fins, long pectoral fins, a crescent shaped caudal fin (tail), paired pelvic fins and an anal fin. The second dorsal fin and the anal fin are smaller than the first dorsal fin. They have large, black eyes, a conical snout and five large gill slits. Their serrated teeth are triangular in shape, and razor sharp. They are colored various forms of grey to bronze on top, with white underneath, with a black blotch known as the axillar patch on the body near where the posterior edge of the pectoral fin joins the body.

Although they are not the largest species of fish in the sea, great whites are the largest fish who hunt large animals. These sharks have been reported to reach some remarkable sizes, some of which cannot be verified. For example, Professor J.L. B. Smith in his book, *The Sea Fishes of Southern Africa*, reported that great whites attained a length of 40 feet. Among the largest of the verifiable specimens was a great white caught in the Mediterranean Sea off Malta back in 1987 that was 23 feet long. Another verified large specimen, this one measuring 21 feet, was caught back in 1945 by a commercial shark fisherman, Alexandro del Valle, off the northern coast of Cuba.

The largest specimen measured off the east coast of the United States was a shark that became tangled in a net near Cape Lookout back in 1918. This fish was measured by shark hunter and researcher Russell Coles, who found the great white to be 22 feet in length.

Like other lamnids, great whites have some unique physical features which help them thrive in cooler waters. These sharks have a complex heat exchange system that allows them to retain much of their body heat, which in turn helps their muscles and vital organs work more efficiently. In cool water, they can move rapidly and efficiently on a moment's notice.

Though not as fast as other lamnids such as shortfin makos, great whites are capable of traveling at high rates of speed. They normally swim at about 2 miles per hour, but when in attack mode they can travel up to ten times as fast.

When attacking, a great white uses its speed and weight to build up the force necessary to carve out meat from its large victims, which frequently include loggerhead turtles, large fish, birds, and marine mammals such as sea lions, seals, whales, dolphins or porpoises. Sometimes, when practical, great whites swallow their prey whole.

From the coast of North Carolina south to the Florida Keys, great whites tend to stay well offshore in the cooler, deeper water, out near the edge of the continental shelf. But when water temperatures drop in the winter, they sometimes come close inshore. Certain combinations of weather and tides can also produce conditions that bring the great whites in from the deep during the warmer months.

Because of their preference for cooler water, great whites are rarely seen near shore along the coast of the southeastern United States, but when they are observed, they often cause quite a stir. In this area, they are most frequently seen in the vicinity of Cape Lookout and the southern end of the Outer Banks of North Carolina. But as this book shows, these amazing apex predators have been encountered all along this stretch of coast, from Currituck to Cumberland Island.

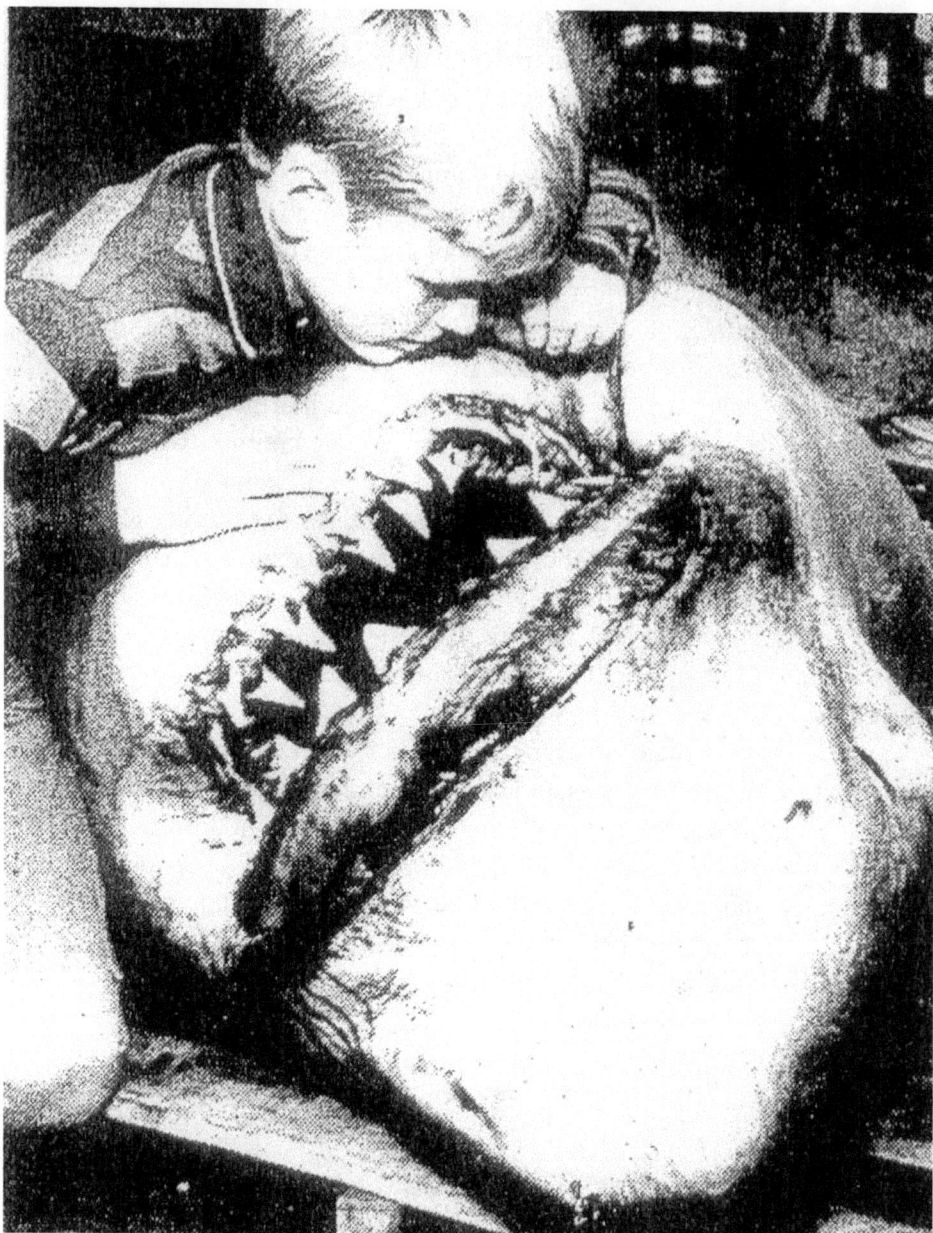

Jon Dodrill imspects the great white shark his father captured while aboard the **Alligator** *in September 1984. (Photo courtesy Jon Dodrill)*

1
EARLY ENCOUNTERS WITH
GREAT WHITES

Great white sharks have been swimming in the waters off what is today the southeastern United States for millions of years. Evidence of this can be found in eastern North Carolina at places such as Aurora, where fossil collectors come to search for the remains of plants and animals that were deposited in the distant past. Countless numbers of teeth from great white sharks have been dug up from these ancient marine deposits, and are on display in places such as the Aurora Fossil Museum, the North Carolina Museum of Natural History in Raleigh, and scores of private collections around the world. All give mute testimony to the fact that great whites have been swimming and hunting in our waters for eons.

Native Americans in what is now the southeastern United States certainly knew of the great white sharks. We know this because remains of these sharks have been found by archaeologists in mounds and middens of the region, from Lake Okeechobee, Biscayne Bay and Sanibel Island in Florida to as far north as the Etowah Mound in the Appalachian Mountains of northern Georgia.

One question that is often debated is exactly how did the Indians capture large pelagic fish, including great white sharks? Some theorize that the captures were opportunistic in nature, resulting from Indians scavenging a fish carcass that washed up on the beach. Another school of thought holds that the Indians caught them using nets, wooden clubs or wooden hooks in offshore waters.

Archaeologist Lewis Larson, who studied the various methods employed by the Native Americans in procuring food in the southeastern

US, noted that we should not be surprised to find remains of white sharks in the archaeological sites across the region. "C. Carcharius is not one of the more common sharks in the Southeast," he wrote. "Nevertheless, it is found with enough frequency so that the presence of teeth from this species at southeastern archaeological sites need not be regarded as an unusual circumstance."

Despite the fact that these remarkable fish have been here for so long, it was nearly three hundred years after the Carolina coast was explored and settled before their presence was noted here. The first documented capture of one of these large sharks occurred less than 120 years ago in the waters just off Shackelford Banks, a short distance offshore from the Cape Lookout Lighthouse.

For many years of the early twentieth century there were shark fishing stations set up along these shores. One of the most famous shark hunters to work at one of these stations was the aforementioned Russell Coles, who had several memorable encounters with a variety of large sharks, including great whites. He has the distinction of observing and measuring the largest great white documented in the waters off the southeastern United States, a 22 footer he found tangled in a net just off Cape Lookout back in June of 1918.

But the honor of the first documented capture of a great white along this coast does not belong to the shark hunters. That honor goes instead to Captain Lorenzo Willis and his crew of shore based whalers who harpooned a memorable white shark off Cape Lookout in early May of 1888.

The Willis family of Carteret County has a long tradition of making their living from the seas along the southern Outer Banks of North Carolina. In days gone by, this family was renowned for producing some of the most expert fishermen and whalers in the region. It should come as no surprise that a member of this family that spent so much of their time on the water should be involved in what is so far the earliest known account of the capture of a great white shark along the Carolina coast.

In the 18th and 19th centuries, people who lived along the barrier islands from Bear Island in Onslow County up the Outer Banks to Cape Hatteras maintained a whaling industry that has long since ceased to exist. To supplement their fishing income, many hardy souls along this stretch of coast put to sea in pursuit of whales. Unlike the New England brand of whaling, the whaling in North Carolina was shore based. Lookouts were posted along the high dunes to scan the horizon for whales. When one was spotted, a signal was given, and crews of men converged on the scene to put out to sea in pursuit of these whales.

The whalers put out to sea in wooden whaleboats propelled by oars. They rowed on the open ocean, sometimes for many miles, until they caught up with the whale, then the harpooner would let fly with his harpoons, and, if all went well, they killed their prey. The whale's carcass was then towed back to shore, where the animal was processed for oil, whalebone and any other commodity the inhabitants could get from their prize.

Captain Lorenzo Willis and his men were members of one of the whaling and fishing communities that once existed along the Shackleford Banks in Carteret County. At one time, there were settlements of several hundred inhabitants, including women and children, who lived within sight of the Cape Lookout Lighthouse. But after a period of rather intense hurricanes in the late 1800's, the inhabitants moved from this exposed location to places that provided more protection from the elements.

On a cool morning in May of 1888, Captain Willis and his crew were working in the waters just east of Cape Lookout. Whether they had been called out in pursuit of a whale that got away, or were just cruising about hoping to get something by chance, is unknown. As they worked their way along the coast, they came to a landmark known as Wreck Point, the tip of the sandy spit that stretches west from Cape Lookout back toward Shackleford Banks. The waters contained between Wreck Point and the Shackleford Banks are called Lookout Bight, or simply The Bight.

A short distance off Wreck Point, one of the crewman spotted a large animal swimming in the water. With the expert guidance provided by their captain, the experienced crew maneuvered their craft into position, and the harpooner let fly his weapon. The throw struck its mark. We can only imagine what surprise Captain Willis and his crew felt when they realized their target was no mere whale. Instead, an enormous shark with a mouth full of razor sharp teeth jumped clear out of the water. A fierce struggle between man and fish ensued.

Willis and his crew battled this shark for more than two hours. They were fortunate that the animal was in relatively shallow water and did not have the opportunity to dive deeper than the length of their rope. We don't know exactly how he did it, but the harpooner was finally able to kill the huge fish after a long, desperate fight.

The shark was secured to their whaleboat and towed ashore, where Captain Willis and his men hoped to learn more about their strange catch.

They found it to be 18 feet long, and 8 feet wide across its pectorals. They claimed that the shark weighed two tons, but whether this was an accurate measurement or an educated guess is unknown.

After measuring the shark, the whalers decided to dissect its body. Inside the shark's stomach, they found the remains of 6 sharks, the smallest of which measured 6 feet long.

"His mouth was large enough to roll a kerosene barrel into with room to spare," wrote an unnamed correspondent for the newspaper in the nearby town of Beaufort. "He had three rows of teeth, one inch wide and two inches long. Our oldest fisherman pronounced him to be the largest ever killed on our coast."

Fishermen along the Carolina coast in those days did not differentiate sharks by species the way we do today. Instead, they grouped them in such descriptive categories as "hammerheads" or "maneaters." Thus, sharks were not broken down into the various orders and species with which we are now familiar. It is doubtful if Captain Willis or any of his men on the beach that day back in 1888 realized the significance of their catch, or ever knew the true identity of the shark they had hauled in.

Although Captain Willis never claimed what kind of shark they had caught, it is possible to conclude that it was a great white thanks to a number of factors. First, we can narrow down the list of possible sharks based on size. Of the nearly sixty species of sharks that are found off the Carolinas, there are only four types of sharks that cruise along the surface of the water near the North Carolina coast large enough to have been the one caught by Captain Willis-tiger sharks, great whites, whale sharks and basking sharks.

This group can be narrowed down further based on diet. Whale sharks and basking sharks grow to extremely large size, but unlike other shark species their bodies and teeth have adapted to a diet of plankton and krill, much like a baleen whale. One would not find, "6 large sharks" inside either a whale shark or a basking shark.

Tiger sharks 18 feet in length do prowl along the North Carolina coast, but they are not known to reach such large dimensions as 8 feet across the pectorals, nor do they weigh two tons. According to the International Game Fish Association, the largest tiger shark ever taken in the world on rod and reel was caught by Walter Maxwell near the North Carolina/South Carolina border in 1964. It measured 20 feet long, and weighed 1,780 pounds, an IGFA all tackle world record.

The description of the shark's teeth narrow the shark's identity further. Neither whale sharks nor basking sharks would have "three rows of teeth, one inch wide and two inches long." Nor would teeth from a tiger shark match such a description, as their teeth are curved, much like the teeth of a circular saw. Teeth such as those described by the eyewitness at Beaufort would only be found in one large shark species along the Carolina coast— the great white.

Besides the description of the shark itself, it is important to take into account local weather conditions at the time. The weather in early May of 1888 was described as being unusually cold, with strong winds out of the north, not the conditions that would normally appeal to tiger sharks. Great whites are known to thrive in the more temperate waters, and one could expect to find them in these cool waters instead of the tiger sharks, which are more likely to be along the Carolina coast in the summer months.

Historically, white sharks have been more prevalent in these waters in spring and fall than at other times of the year. However, great whites have been documented in the waters off North Carolina in every month, from January through December.

During a recent conversation with Dr. Frank Schwartz of the University of North Carolina's Institute of Marine Sciences at Morehead City, he confirmed that great whites have been spotted several times in the spring in the vicinity of Cape Lookout. "We had a couple of big ones spotted on some wrecks just on the other side of the Lookout Shoals back in 2001 and 2002," he said. "But the little ones, the eight footers, I see in April here off Beaufort Inlet and Shackleford Banks."

According to Dr. Schwartz, the largest great white taken along the North Carolina coast in recent years was caught approximately 20 miles south of Beaufort Inlet in April of 1986 by some longline fishermen out of Morehead City. This shark measured 15 feet nine inches long, and weighed 2143.26 pounds.

From the descriptions of the shark that were penned at the time by the unnamed correspondent who saw the shark and spoke with its captors, we can conclude that Captain Willis and his men off the Shackleford Banks did indeed catch a great white. This is the only known species of large sharks with rows of large, triangular teeth that prefers cool, temperate waters and is a regular visitor to the southern Outer Banks in the spring.

Down through the years, there have been several memorable encounters with great white sharks along the coast from Currituck south to the Cape Fear. Though new accounts are surfacing as we learn more about the ocean, Captain Willis' shark remains the earliest great white captured and documented in the waters off North Carolina.

This great white shark was caught off the Outer Banks in May 1984. (N.C. Department of Archives and History.)

2
MONSTER GREAT WHITE
OFF THE
OUTER BANKS?

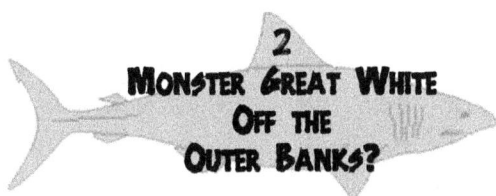

Great whites are among the largest species of fish in the sea. Although many scientists today discount claims that these sharks reach sizes bigger than 30 feet in length, there have been some claims of great whites reaching truly monstrous sizes, even off the southeastern coast of the United States.

Aycock Brown, who spent much of his life promoting the Outer Banks of North Carolina, used to relate a story about a huge great white measuring 30 feet long that was hooked near the Gulf Stream off Cape Lookout in the early 20th century. This shark was so big that it could not be hauled aboard the commercial shark fishing boat that caught it. Brown stated that the fishermen saved some of the teeth, which measured a remarkable 4 inches long.

Glenn Reed, once the proprietor of a popular Myrtle Beach attraction known as "Shark's Tooth Cove," has studied sharks and shark's teeth for many years. He finds claims of 4-inch teeth from a modern great white hard to believe.

"We've heard a lot of tales about the sizes of teeth and the exaggerated sizes basically boil down to just fish stories, because the tooth configuration rule of thumb measurement is 1 inch of tooth represents approximately 10 feet of shark," notes Reed. "The largest shark tooth I've ever seen, and I've traveled the world looking for sharks, especially great whites, was 2 7/8 inches. That's the largest."

Based on this rule of thumb measurement, a 4-inch long tooth would have to come from a shark measuring in the neighborhood of 40 feet long. Although there have been unsubstantiated claims of great whites which were that big, none has ever been confirmed.

Even as some people contend that great whites have been caught that were nearly 40 feet in length, scientists view such claims as mere sea legends. Controversy and contention surrounds the whole topic of largest great white ever taken, with many scientists using arcane formulae and complicated calculations to tear down one case and build up another.

After studying the sizes of bites inflicted upon whale carcasses off southern Australia, shark expert John Randall concluded in 1973 that white sharks, "as long as 25 or 26 feet (7 1/2 or 8 meters) exist today."

The largest great whites ever reported were truly remarkable fish. One specimen from False Bay, South Africa, was reportedly 43 feet long. Another large shark, this one caught in 1930, was taken off Grand Manan Island in the Bay of Fundy between New Brunswick and Nova Scotia. This shark was reputed to be 36 1/2 feet long. The size of these enormous sharks was never independently verified, and has been disputed by researchers down through the years.

In the late 1950's, fishermen aboard the boat *Golden Bells* hooked an enormous great white while fishing in the Indian Ocean near the isle of Silhouette in the Seychelles. After a long struggle, the giant shark was hauled alongside the vessel but it eventually managed to escape. As the shark passed under the boat, the crew was able to get an idea of just how big the shark was. "When its snout lay exactly under the rudder I raised my arm so that Ton Milot, who had scurried up to the bows to mark the position of the tail, was able to plumb-bob its nether extremity," wrote Captain William Travis. "At this signal he peered over the side, edged a little further forward and then made a decisive scratch across the bulwark with his knife. The point at which he did so was exactly three feet from the stem of the boat. Our shark measured twenty-nine feet in length!"

The longest accurately measured and independently verified great white ever recorded in the world was taken off the coast of Malta in 1987. It measured 23 feet long.

A couple of possible great whites were encountered off Charleston, South Carolina over 160 years ago which may have been of record setting proportions. In 1901, Captain William O. Ferguson recalled several shark attacks in the Charleston area of which he had knowledge from his many years of residence in that city and working on the sea off the southeastern US coast. One attack he noted, which occurred circa 1840, involved a sailor who was knocked into the waters of Charleston Harbor and killed by what witnesses claim was a 25-foot shark. A few years prior to that episode, a 25-foot long shark was killed in the vicinity of Charleston which contained the remains of some unfortunate sailor, identifiable because part of his uniform was still intact when the contents of the shark's stomach were examined.

Because so little was recorded about either shark, we cannot say unequivocally that either was a great white. But if the 25 feet in length Captain Ferguson claimed was even close to accurate, the list of potential sharks is narrowed to only one. There is only one known species of shark which grows to over 20 feet in length that consumes mammals such as humans off the Carolina coast, and that is the great white.

The longest independently verified and accurately measured great white taken along the coast of the southeastern United States in recent years was the shark taken by Joel Prouty and company during commercial shark fishing operations aboard the *Ms. Manana* off Key Largo, Florida, in 1997. This shark was 17 feet long. Since the ban on catching great whites has been instituted, it is doubtful that any larger specimens will be landed in the near future. Still, there are reports of great whites being seen off the coast from Florida to the Carolinas that eclipse these specimens actually landed.

The reason the really monstrous great whites have been seen and not landed is uncertain. It could be due to the fact that since fishermen normally use fish to catch fish, the bait is of little or no interest to the really big sharks. These mature great whites are believed by many reputable authorities to prefer meat from sources with high fat and caloric content, such as large mammals like whales, or even fish like other large sharks.

The type of equipment used by shark fishermen also has much to do with why really large great whites are only infrequently caught. Shark expert Stewart Springer reasoned that the equipment used by fishermen was inadequate to land such powerful sharks. He pointed out that the big ones that had been landed were taken accidentally, and were the result of the large great white becoming entangled in a line and caught with multiple hooks.

To add to all of this confusion over size, sometimes large sharks are misidentified. Many people who have seen what they believe to be a truly enormous great white have in some cases been looking at a basking shark. These sharks are the second largest fish in the ocean, after the whale shark, growing in excess of 30 feet long. When seen from above, they are often hard to differentiate from a great white. Basking sharks are frequently seen on the surface of the ocean off the Carolinas, Georgia and Florida during the winter months.

Nonetheless, there are cases of people encountering huge sharks they report as being in excess of 20 feet long off the coast of the southeastern United States that have been verified by experts to be great whites. So until our knowledge of the seas is more complete, it is impossible to assign a maximum size for a great white shark in the Atlantic or any other ocean.

Whether Brown's shark was a truly remarkable shark or merely a legend of the seas will never be known.

This great white shark was encountered off the Outer Banks near Rodanthe by fishermen aboard the sportfishing vessel **Poacher** *on May 13, 2004. (Photo: Captain Charles Perry)*

3
GREAT WHITES OF THE
NORTHERN OUTER BANKS

M y God, Devon, that's a great white!" exclaimed Captain Charles Perry as he looked down from the deck of the charter boat *Poacher* upon the surface of the ocean where a large shark was swimming alongside their vessel just a few miles off Rodanthe, on the North Carolina Outer Banks. As a man with an intimate knowledge of the marine world, Perry understood as few others could grasp just how unique and fortunate he and his friends were to have the opportunity to see such an animal in the wild.

A world renowned marlin fisherman, Perry is a seasoned mariner with decades of experience fishing the world's oceans. A native of the Outer Banks, he grew up fishing and boating in these waters before traveling further afield in search of fishing adventures. He has seen some remarkable fish in his day, including tiger sharks and hammerheads. He even had a thrilling encounter with a great white one night off the coast of Australia. But few of his adventures could top the thrill of witnessing this massive great white in the waters off North Carolina.

On this warm spring day, May 13th, 2004, he sailed out of Oregon Inlet for a trip with his friend, Captain Devon Cage, aboard the latter's 41' sportfishing boat. They were headed south towards Cape Hatteras, keeping an eye out for signs of cobia swimming along the surface of the sea. Perry was along more for the opportunity to be on the sea and enjoy the company of his friend, and not stalking the large marlin. He was not expecting to find any really large fish.

They originally sailed just offshore, but turned and headed further out to sea due to visibility problems. Approximately 13 miles from shore, something unusual caught Cage's eye. He thought at first that it was perhaps a cobia, but then realized it was a shark of some kind. But the distance between the two fins protruding above the water indicated something much larger than a mako or a sandtiger, sharks one might expect to encounter along the Outer Banks. They made a slight detour to investigate.

As they approached the mysterious creature, they began to get a good look at what it was. Soon, they realized the identity of the large fish. "When we got where we could see I said, 'My God, Devon, that's a great white!'" recalled Perry. "We could pull right up to it, and it would look at the boat, and swim right by it."

The men scurried to the tower of the *Poacher* to get a better view of the shark. "It swam by the stern of the boat a couple of different times," said Perry. "We could see the size of it as compared to the stern of the boat and we felt like it was very likely 16 to 18 feet long, probably closer to 18 feet at least. We knew how wide the boat was, which is like 15 feet 8 inches, and when it went across the stern of the boat, there was a lot of fish on each side of the boat when it was straight across the stern. We saw this a couple of different times."

While the men from the *Poacher* found the length of the great white to be notable, they found the girth of the shark to be especially impressive. "We knew the fish was large, and as we looked at the fish straight down on it, I don't think there was any doubt it was 4 feet across its body," noted Perry. "I feel like it was probably pregnant. It was so fat that it had to be pregnant, or else it just had the biggest feed of its life." Perry has shown video footage he took of the shark to several scientists in California who are familiar with great whites in the Pacific Ocean. Most agree that the shark appears to be pregnant, and very likely gave birth soon after the incident.

"We didn't see the young being had," said Perry, "but I feel like the shark was very likely pregnant and in that water temperature (72° F) looking for a temperature right to have the young."

The northern Outer Banks of North Carolina and the Virginia shore lie along the southern end of a stretch of coast known as the Mid Atlantic Bight. This is the name given to the long stretch of coast lying between Cape Cod, Massachusetts and Cape Hatteras, North Carolina.

Scientists John Casey and Harold Pratt studied great white sharks in the western North Atlantic, and found these sharks to be relatively abundant in the Mid Atlantic Bight. "From all available evidence the white shark is more abundant on the continental shelf between Cape Hatteras and Cape Cod (35° 00' N, 43° 00' N) then in any other region in the Western North Atlantic," they wrote. "More young white sharks have been caught there than in any area of comparable size in the world."

Despite being on the southern portion of this area with a reputation for a relative abundance of great whites, reports of sightings of these large sharks are rare along the stretch of coast from Cape Hatteras to Cape Henry. Although parts of this coast have been sparsely populated, this lack of great white sightings cannot be accounted for by the absence of humans on the water. This portion of the Outer Banks has been explored and settled since the 1500's, and Chesapeake Bay is one of the most heavily traveled bodies of water in the United States, with ships from all nations plying the bay headed for ports such as Norfolk, Virginia or Baltimore, Maryland.

Remarkably, the earliest documented encounter with a great white in the waters off Virginia occurred fairly recently. On June 6th, 1981, Fred Williams of Richmond caught a great white while fishing with rod-and-reel on the Southeast Lumps off Virginia Beach. The shark measured 6 feet long, and weighed 131 pounds. The girth of the shark was 37 inches. Claude Bain, director of the Virginia Saltwater Fishing Tournament, readily acknowledges that the size of the record setting fish is far below what one might expect for a great white shark. "Obviously, this is a small fish but is still the only one to be landed on a rod-and-reel in Virginia," he notes.

There have been several other great whites caught along the southeastern Virginia coast, just not with a rod and reel, therefore they do not qualify for the record. Three of these sharks were taken from these waters in the first two week of November in the year 2000. The first was a six footer caught near Virginia Beach. This shark was given to the Virginia Institute of Marine Science, where scientists studied the rare catch.

A week later, two great whites were caught in a net near Virginia Beach. Dan McCulloch and his crew were bringing in their nets about half a mile from shore off Sandbridge when they noticed they had captured something really large. They found two sharks that had apparently been feeding on sea bass trapped in the net, and gotten themselves tangled up in the process.

McCulloch's crew hauled the first big shark, which they originally thought was a mako, on board. After further investigation, it was determined that instead of a mako, they had landed an 11 foot great white. Scientists later confirmed the identity of the shark.

But this was only half the story, for the other shark tangled in the net was also a great white. This one was even larger than the other. McCulloch estimated that it was, "twice as large," as the first one. Unfortunately, the opportunity to accurately measure the huge shark never presented itself.

As they pulled the huge shark alongside the boat, they got a close up view of their remarkable catch. "When we went to poke at it, he or she rolled an eyeball at us that was as big as a softball, black," McCulloch said.

After being prodded, the large shark recovered its senses and came to life. The great white rolled out of the net, and swam away, disappearing into the depths of the sea.

Four years later, on November 1st, 2004, another great white was caught off the Virginia coast. A fisherman off Virginia Beach inadvertently caught this one in a net. The shark was taken to the Virginia Beach Seafood Company where manager John Galloway got a good look at the shark. "It was a young great white," he noted, "and it only weighed 115 pounds, and measured 5 feet long. One of the boys caught him in a gill net just off Virginia Beach. He was fishing for spots and croakers, and found the shark in his net, already dead."

The shark did not stay in Virginia Beach long, as agents with the National Marine Fisheries Service arrived on the scene and took the shark into custody. This caused a small stir, as there is no law against catching great white sharks in Virginia Commonwealth waters. State quota laws there regulate the amount of fish in the generic category of sharks, and make no differentiation among species. Thus there is no law against landing a great white, as long as it is done within three miles of shore, in Virginia's territorial waters.

Captain Cage of the *Poacher* is fully aware of the rarity of sightings of great whites in the vicinity of Oregon Inlet. "The only other confirmed great whites that I have heard of out of Oregon Inlet came from net fisherman," he said. "I know several guys who have caught 500 pounders in their dogfish nets in the winter. I also know a longline captain who said he has seen them off here in the winter near the Gulf Stream. But I also talked to captains who have fished here for 40 years and they said they have never seen one, nor remember anyone having an encounter like I did on a charter boat out of Oregon Inlet ever. In my 20 years here as a captain, I never remember anyone ever seeing one confirmed."

The shark they observed that warm day in May continued on its course, undeterred by the presence of the fishing boat and its curious human passengers. After several minutes, Cage decided to part company with the shark, and headed his vessel back out toward the east. "We stayed with the great white for 10 minutes maybe, but when I left her she was still on top," recalled Cage. "I think I could have stayed with her for miles really by the way it was acting. I haven't seen any other great whites since and really doubt that I ever will. But next year in May, when water temperature gets to be 72°, I'm going to go back out in the area and have a look."

The last time they saw the shark, it was headed west, toward Rodanthe and the beaches of the Cape Hatteras National Seashore.

This juvenile shark was caught off Cape Lookout by Russell Coles in 1918. (National Marine Fisheries Service)

4
GREAT WHITE SHARKS
OFF THE SOUTHERN OUTER BANKS

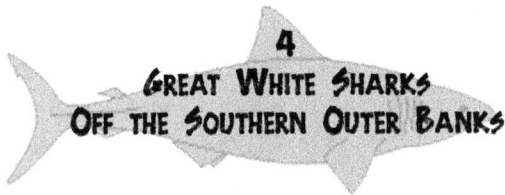

In the early 20th century, there were several thrilling encounters with great whites in the waters off the southern Outer Banks of NorthCarolina. Many of these were chronicled by Russell J. Coles, who spent much of his time hunting for sharks and rays in the waters off Cape Lookout in the first quarter of the 20th century. Even today, at the dawn of the 21st century, scientists owe a huge debt to Coles for the work he did documenting the various species of sharks he personally observed.

The largest great white ever recorded along the southeastern United States was examined and measured by Coles. On June 28th, 1918, he came across a large great white that had been tangled in a net near Cape Lookout. Earlier, some other fishermen had reported seeing an enormous shark entangled in a fishing net just offshore, but when they said the shark was as big as their 25-foot fishing boat, Coles dismissed their story as a tall tale.

Upon closer investigation, he found the fishermen's description of the large shark remarkably accurate. "My carefully noted observations justify the following claim of dimensions for it," wrote Coles. "length, 22 ft.; head, larger than 50 gallon barrel; mouth , 3 ft. wide; circumference at arm-pit of pectoral, 18 ft.; length of pectoral, 6 ft.; width of pectoral, 3 1/2 ft.; dorsal, not seen; width at caudal notch, origin of tail, 20 in.; width of tail, 7 ft.; weight, over 2 tons."

Coles led an adventurous life. Often armed with a harpoon and a long knife, he prowled the waters near Cape Lookout and the Shackleford Banks on his quest for sharks. On numerous occasions, his fishing trips turned dangerous.

One incident took place back in 1903 in the Cape Lookout Bight. He was out harpooning turtles when a great white estimated to be 18 feet long made several threatening moves towards his small skiff. Armed on this occasion with a big knife, a harpoon and a high-powered rifle, Coles watched warily as the huge shark sized up his small boat.

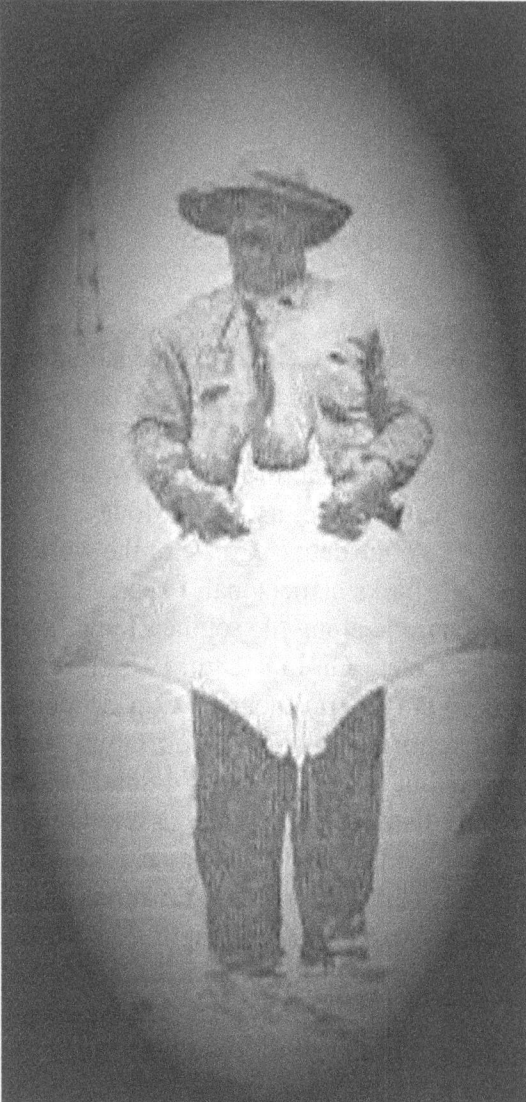

Pioneer shark researcher Russeell Coles.
(National Marine Fisheries Service)

The great white retreated about a hundred yards before turning and making what Coles was sure was its final charge in for the kill. But before the shark reached its prey, it veered off at the last second and took a loggerhead turtle instead.

Coles later said of the incident, "I am convinced that this shark had satisfied himself that I was suitable food and had only retired to acquire speed for leaping into the skiff and seizing me, and that the coming to the surface of the turtle at that instant was all that saved me from a dangerous, knife and shagreen fight."

Two years later, Coles had a similar episode with what he believed to be a great white, this one measuring an estimated 20 feet long. As with his earlier adventure, the timely arrival of a loggerhead turtle captured the shark's attention and ended the encounter before anyone got hurt (except the turtle of course). Next day, Coles harpooned this turtle, and found teeth marks thirty inches wide left behind by the shark. The shark managed to tear away the hapless loggerhead's right rear flipper and a part of his shell.

Nearly a decade later, Coles had another dangerous run in with a great white in the Cape Lookout Bight. This was by far his most perilous adventure, and nearly ended in the shark hunter's demise.

After trying to lure a great white he had spotted into shallow water, Coles jumped out of his boat and pushed the small craft about a hundred yards away from where he was standing. Secured to his boat with a rope, armed with a harpoon, and wading in 5 feet of water, he decided to tempt the great white shark even further by throwing pieces of crushed up fish into the water.

The shark, which up until then had paid scant attention to Coles, could no longer resist the human's dinner invitation. From a half mile away, the scent of the fish remains drew the shark literally into Coles' grasp. Moving with unexpected speed, the great white charged Coles from about a hundred feet.

The redoubtable Coles was ready, and he met the charging great white with a blow from his harpoon. He described what happened next.

"I met the onrushing shark by hurling my harpoon clear to the socket into it, near the angle of the jaw, and as the iron entered its flesh, the shark leaped forward, catching me in the angle formed by its head and the harpoon handle, which caught me just under the right arm, bruising me badly, while my face and neck were somewhat lacerated by coming in contact with the rough hide of the side of its head. As my right arm was free, it was a great chance for using the heavy knife, with which I was armed, had my tackle been strong; but the force of the blow snapped the poorly-made harpoon at the socket and the shark escaped, although it carried its death wound. I never again employed the same black-smith to forge my harpoons, but that poorly-made iron surely brought to a sudden ending a most exciting situation."

History and marine science owe quite a debt to this hapless blacksmith, for it is certain that had the poorly constructed harpoon not broken and allowed the great white to escape, Coles would not have survived the encounter. As a result, Coles would not have lived to publish his fascinating and valuable accounts of his adventures with the large sharks off Cape Lookout.

Though surely stimulating adventures, exploits such as Coles' with great whites along the shores of North Carolina are unheard of today. After the passing of Coles, reports of great whites became few and far between. The reason for this is uncertain, though it may have had more to do with the efforts of mid-twentieth century tourism promoters than with the absence of the sharks.

Half a century passed before another white shark was documented in these waters. In April of 1974, a group of marine scientists were longlining for sharks just off the Shackleford Banks between Cape Lookout and Beaufort Inlet. This turned out to be one of their more significant fishing trips along this stretch of coast, for in addition to the more commonly encountered sharks such as hammerhead sharks, sandbar sharks and sandtiger sharks, they managed to hook a great white.

This shark was not significant for its size. It was a juvenile male, with a total length of just over five feet (1967 mm). Instead, this shark was important because of who caught it. For the first time since the passing of Coles, scientists were present when a great white shark was caught in the waters off North Carolina.

"At that time, that was the first documented confirmed record besides some of the earlier records of Russell Coles back in the early 1900's," said Dr. Steven W. Ross, who was one of the scientists present when this great white shark was landed. "The significance of that record is that the animal itself was saved and so the record was validated. The problem with some of the earlier records is that there is no remaining validation, no photographs, no specimens, no jaws. While we trust some of these earlier records, scientists are always looking for validation. So that was the first validated record."

Over thirty years have passed since this great white was landed, and during that time Ross has gone on to become one of the most respected ichthyologists in the region. Whether in a laboratory, on a research vessel or in a bathysphere underneath the depths of the sea, Ross has studied the marine life off our coast as few have. Now a research scientist at the University of North Carolina at Wilmington, he has had ample opportunity to observe sharks in our waters.

The great white landed on that spring day back in 1974 was the first one he ever saw off the Carolina coast, but it would not be the last. Since then, he has had some memorable encounters with great whites.

"I've seen a few others that have been caught occasionally by sport fishermen and commercial fishermen in the area," he recalled. "I encountered a moderate sized great white during one of my research trips just north of Cape Hatteras. I've seen one cruising along the surface as is common to this type of shark. It was probably a six to eight foot shark. It was just north of a place fishermen call, 'The Point.'

"So I have run into a few of them over the years, but they aren't as common as some of the more tropical or inshore sharks."

Dr. Ross is quick to point out that, without question, the most remarkable great white shark he has ever seen was the one landed by his friend off Cape Lookout and brought back to Morehead City in September of 1984.

Great whites are really big fish. To get an idea of just how large these fish are, a person can travel to locales such as South Africa or Australia and pay fairly large sums of money to be placed into a cage and thrown overboard into seas where great whites are known to congregate, there to experience the exhilaration of being attacked by a great white. While these encounters are very photogenic and exciting to watch on television, it should be remembered that most of these incidents are provoked by the guides or skippers placing large amounts of cut up fish, bloody animal remains and other baits to lure the sharks in for the tourists.

A much safer and more economical way to see a great white up close is to visit the North Carolina Maritime Museum at Beaufort. There, hanging from a wall immediately to the left of the entrance doorway, are the stuffed and mounted remains of a 2,080 pound mature male great white that is without question the most famous great white shark ever taken along the North Carolina coast. Though still quite imposing with its menacing teeth bared for all to behold, the display contains only about half of the shark's original 15 and a half feet long body.

Lloyd Davidson, Jon Dodrill and Sylvester Karasinski caught the shark on Tuesday evening, September 25th, 1984. Davidson, captain of the 41' commercial fishing boat *Alligator*, and his crew were fishing approximately 40 miles south of Cape Lookout in 28 fathoms of water. The temperature of the water was approximately 70° F.

The men were long-lining for sharks, and had already pulled in a respectable haul that included several tiger sharks. The great white had been feasting on sharks that had already been hooked, and it became tangled in the line.

Dodrill was at the back of the boat processing the catch as it came aboard. Davidson, who was at the rail on the starboard quarter at the front of the vessel hydraulically retrieving the cable mainline, called out to Dodrill, "Jon, you better come forward and take a look at this."

"I've seen all kinds of sharks," said Dodrill, "but judging from that huge lunate tail, which looked as wide as the flukes of a small whale, I knew it was the biggest I'd ever seen. From the shape of the tail and the size of the shark, I knew it was a massive white shark. The shark was suspended vertically in the water, tail wrapped in the cable mainline. The girth of its white belly was so large it initially completely obscured the head of the shark. It was unbelievable. It was still alive."

Later, they found out exactly how they had captured this rare shark. "The great white had swallowed whole a 6 foot long tiger shark that we had hooked ," observed Dodrill. "It had a hook in its belly, a hook in its mouth, and the tail was wrapped in the cable bottom mainline."

The fishermen wrapped two heavy lines around the base of the shark's tail, cut the cable loose, then tied the shark off to the back of their boat. With their catch thus immobilized, they re-spiked the mainline and finished bringing in the rest of their catch—17 sharks in all including a tiger shark nearly 12 feet long.

The weather was calm, the seas flat and clear. Curiosity got the better of them, and soon Davidson and Dodrill put on their masks and dove overboard to get a better look at the huge shark tied off the back of their vessel.

"The view of this great fish against a late afternoon blue water backdrop was very impressive," recalled Dodrill. "Not wishing to share the view with other curious in water onlookers that might arrive any moment, we didn't stay in the water long!"

Soon, weather conditions started deteriorating as a storm was moving in, so Davidson decided to return to port early. The great white would not fit on the *Alligator*, so they winched as much of it on board as possible, and towed the rest. With their catch thus secured, the *Alligator* returned to port in Morehead City, where she arrived in the wee hours of September 27th, 1984.

Earlier that morning, Dr. Ross had received a telephone call from Davidson's wife alerting him to the fact that the *Alligator* was heading into Morehead City with their remarkable catch. Camera in hand, Ross was at the waterfront when they arrived back in port.

"It was very exciting to see this big shark come into the dock," recalled Ross. "It is not common to encounter great whites in our waters, even though they do show up. This was a pretty amazing fish. At that time that was the largest single fish that had ever been caught in North Carolina waters. The shark was so large they had to use the boatlift there at Russell's Boatworks to lift it out of the water. At that time I photographed the shark with its captors in front of it."

Using a crane to pick it up, the shark was placed in the back of a pickup truck and taken to Davidson's house. Later that morning, following a brief stop at a truck weigh station and a local elementary school, the monstrous shark was taken to Ottis' Fish Market on the waterfront in Morehead City.

The fishermen were surprised at the amount of interest people showed in their shark. As people came from all over the area to see it firsthand, Davidson's great white became something of a media sensation. This was back in the days when the *Jaws* movies were still fresh in people's minds, so many were curious to see one of these creatures up close.

Jon Dodrill, Lloyd Davidson and Sylvester Karasinski of the sharkfishing boat Alligator on the Morehead City dock with the great white shark they caught on September 25, 1984.
(Photo: Dr. Steve Ross, UNC-Wilmington)

The shark's carcass went on display at Ottis' Fish Market in Morehead City, where it remained for the weekend. There, curious onlookers generously donated 50 cents to come by and catch a glimpse of the great white. It was estimated that over 3,500 people visited the Morehead City waterfront to see the rare sight.

At the end of the weekend, Davidson's shark went into a freezer to preserve the fish for future showings. All of the interest in the shark had given him the idea to put the huge shark on display at the North Carolina State Fair in Raleigh.

A special exhibit was built to show the shark at the State Fair. Along with the remains of the shark, drawings and informational handouts were prepared to educate people about great whites and other sharks off the Carolina coast. By the time the fair ended, over 50,000 people had come by to take a look at the great white. Davidson's shark was one of the most popular exhibits at the fair in 1984.

Later, taxidermist Al Swanson of Virginia Beach, Virginia, mounted half of the shark. The Bill Walker family, who owned the trophy, donated it to the North Carolina Maritime Museum in Beaufort. There, it continues to impress the curious who stop by for an up close glimpse of a great white shark.

The presence of great white sharks along the southern Outer Banks of North Carolina is neither widely known nor understood. Basic questions such as where do the great whites live, are they migrating through the area, or do they reside permanently in the deep waters off the continental shelf are yet to be answered. From Beaufort Inlet to Hatteras Inlet, only a few large ones have been reported in recent years, but it is certain that these sharks do still visit the area regularly.

"We know about three big ones, 2 in 2001 and 2002, off on the other side of the shoals," says Dr. Frank Schwartz of the University of North Carolina Marine Science Institute at Morehead City, "and then several years ago we had 15 1/2 footer off the edge of the shelf. But the little ones, the eight footers, I see in April here off Beaufort Inlet."

Dr. Schwartz has spent several decades studying sharks and rays, and is one of the foremost authorities on sharks in Carolina waters. Down through the years he has gathered several accounts of white sharks that have been encountered by fishermen or divers off North Carolina. He notes that three great white shark pups washed up on Ocracoke in May of 1996. How they got there, he says, is a mystery.

That same month, two young great whites were landed just off the Core Banks between Ocracoke and Cape Lookout. On May 3rd, 1996, Glen

Hopkins, a commercial fisherman from Manteo, was fishing for sharks out of Ocracoke when he landed the two great whites.

One of the great whites was caught approximately 1 1/2 miles off Drum Inlet. A larger one was caught a little further offshore, 4 miles off Drum Inlet in 9.9 fathoms of water. The water temperature was 66.7 ° F.

The larger of the two was caught inadvertently after becoming tangled in the line after snagging its dorsal fin on a hook. "It was already dead when we got to it," noted Hopkins. "Otherwise we would have released it."

The smaller of the two was processed shortly after it was taken, and no accurate measurements were made. But the larger one piqued Hopkins' curiosity. He and his crewman hoisted the shark's body onboard and carried it back into Ocracoke.

"The shark was so big we couldn't get it off the boat," said Hopkins. "Fortunately, we found a fellow with a backhoe who helped us haul it up onto the dock."

Word quickly spread around the island about the large great white that was on the dock at the South Point Fish House. People started dropping by to have a look at the spectacle. For many, this was the largest shark they had ever seen in real life.

"Seems there was a fishing tournament going on, so there were more people in Ocracoke than would usually have been there," recalled Hopkins. "The crowd got so big that they had to call in a deputy sheriff to direct traffic."

Hopkins realized that his great white might be of interest to scientists, so he contacted the N. C. Division of Marine Fisheries to report his catch. Jim Francesconi was dispatched from Morehead City to head out to Ocracoke to study the shark.

There was some speculation that the shark was a pregnant female, which would have been a significant find in the Atlantic Ocean. However, after a thorough examination of the shark's remains, Francesconi determined that although it was indeed a female, she was not pregnant.

Upon measuring the shark, Francesconi found her to have a total length of 3240 mm, or approximately 10 1/2 feet long. He then cut up the shark, carefully measuring the various body parts. The liver alone weighed 200 pounds. When finished, he concluded that the shark's total weight was 875 pounds.

"This was an immature female great white that didn't appear to be in the best of health," observed Francesconi. "She didn't have a pretty set of

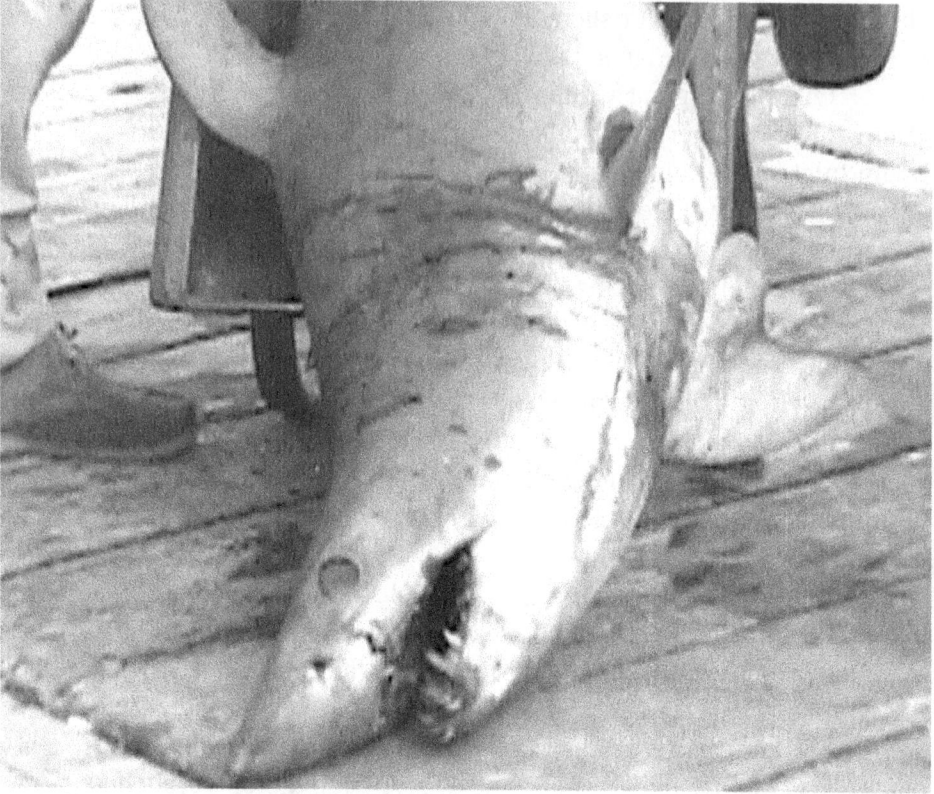

This juvenile white shark was caught near the wreck of the Atlas tanker in 1980. (Photo: Dr. Frank Schwartz, UNC)

jaws, and was missing several teeth. The shark had some interesting parasites on its tail."

These were not the only great whites taken along the southern Outer Banks in 1996. In January of that year, a fisherman landed a young great white approximately 20 miles south of Cape Lookout. This one turned out to be an immature female just over 5 feet long. The remains of this shark were donated to the Florida Museum of Natural History in Gainesville.

Fishermen aren't the only ones who have encountered great whites in these waters. Divers exploring shipwrecks about 40 miles south of Ocracoke have observed great whites on at least two occasions recently, in the summer of 2000 and again in the summer of 2001.

The first incident occurred in the summer of 2000, at the site of the wreck of the tanker *Atlas*, about 15 miles east of Cape Lookout. The wreck is the remains of a 430' long tanker that was sunk by a German U-boat in World War II. On April 9th, 1942, torpedoes from the U-552 struck the tanker, which was loaded with gasoline. A spectacular fire ensued and as a result the ship sank.

The wreck of the *Atlas* sits on the bottom of the ocean in approximately 125 feet of water. Those who are technically able to dive in the strong currents are rewarded with the sighting of a multitude of sea life.

On August 5th, 2000, two dive boats from Discovery Diving, Inc., in Beaufort, brought divers to the site for a visit to the *Atlas*. As the two boats, *Captain's Lady* and *Sea Quest II*, were setting their anchors and making preparations for the dive, those on board spotted a large shark swimming on the surface. A couple of the divers were able to make some photos of the big shark. Copies of these were later given to Dr. Schwartz, who verified the shark as a great white.

Another great white was spotted the following summer in the same general area. This great white was spotted over the site of the wreck of the *Caribsea*, just 5 miles north of the *Atlas*.

The *Caribsea* was a 251' freighter that was the victim of a German U-boat in World War II. Two torpedoes fired from the U-158 on March 11th, 1942 sank this ship. The vessel went down in less than three minutes after being hit, taking 21 of the 28 crewmen on board to a watery grave. This freighter lies on the bottom of the ocean in 85 feet of water less than a dozen miles from the South Core Banks and the Cape Lookout National Seashore. Many divers visit the wreck in hopes of seeing sand tiger sharks which frequently congregate here.

The morning of July 21st, 2001 was sunny and warm. Two boats carried divers out to the *Caribsea* that morning, the *Midnight Express* out of Morehead City and the *Outrageous V* out of Beaufort. They were anchored about 50 yards apart. Clear waters and good visibility rewarded the divers who explored the wreck that day.

At approximately 10:45 a.m., a great white shark came swimming into the area. For the next 20 minutes, the large shark circled the diveboats. One of the divers on board the *Outrageous V* was Dale Boyd of Atlanta, Georgia. He and his dive buddies had driven over nine hours in order to dive the wrecks off the North Carolina coast. They were hoping to have a close encounter with the sandtiger sharks that frequent these waters, and were not expecting to see a great white shark. "From my vantage point I saw a huge fin approach the back of the *Midnight Express*, Olympus Dive Shop's boat that was anchored just behind out starboard stern," recalled Boyd. "I'm not sure why, maybe because I had just read about the great white sighting here

The remains of the shark caught by Davidson and his crew are on display at the North Carolina Maritime Museum in Beaufort.

last year, but somehow I knew what I was seeing. Sure enough there she was, a twelve to fifteen foot great white cruising around our boats."

Nearly all the divers from the *Midnight Express* had returned to their dive boat when the dive master noticed a great white swimming off the back of the boat. Scott Keen, one of the divers on board, was impressed with the shark. "The white shark we saw looked like a torpedo with the mouth on the sides of the snout. She was right under the surface and her dorsal fin would occasionally cut through the top of the perfectly blue water as if to remind us what we were looking at. Seeing that dorsal fin seemed unreal, like something you'd expect from a movie."

The shark gave those on board the dive boat a good opportunity to observe it as it swam back and forth. "The captain figured it was about 15 feet long, as long as the width of the transom," recalled Keen. "The shark got right alongside our dive boat, circling it several times. She would occasionally swim back to the drift line and ball hanging back about 30 yards from the stern of the boat. At the end of a normal dive, divers would ascend from their dive and catch the drift line and work their way hand-over-hand slowly towards the boat."

After a few tense moments, the folks on board the dive boat saw bubbles appear on the surface, the first signs that their friends were returning. With Captain Bobby Purifoy providing cover with a spear gun, the divers were collected back on board the vessel. "You could see the look of terror on their faces through their masks. Everyone on board shouted, 'Hurry! Hurry!' but were quickly silenced by the crew, 'Stop! You'll make them panic!'" Shortly after all the divers were back aboard the *Midnight Express*, the great white swam away.

"For a shark lover this was incredible, I never dreamed I would see a great white in North Carolina waters," Boyd observed. "And as much as I wanted to get into the water to get some video I realize that probably would not have been one of the smartest things I've done in my life. What I got from the boat was too cool, I can only dream what it could have been."

Glen Hopkins caught this great white off Drum Inlet in 1996. (Photo: Jim Francesconi, N.C. Div. of Marine Fisheries)

The sharks that visited these two shipwrecks provided these divers with a rare glimpse of a great white shark in the wild in the waters off the North Carolina coast. Their adventure gives them membership in an elite group, for they joined the long line of people dating back more than 125 years who have had encounters with great white sharks off the southern Outer Banks.

Unfortunately, the exhilaration of seeing a great white in person was tempered by the fact that two of their diving companions were still in the water diving on the wreck 80 feet below. In an effort to warn the unsuspecting divers, the crew wrote a terse message on a piece of slate, "Great White Shark—No Kidding." They then attached the slate and a spear gun to the ship's anchor line and slid it down into the ocean. The divers, it was hoped, would see the message as they made their ascent, following the anchor line back to the boat.

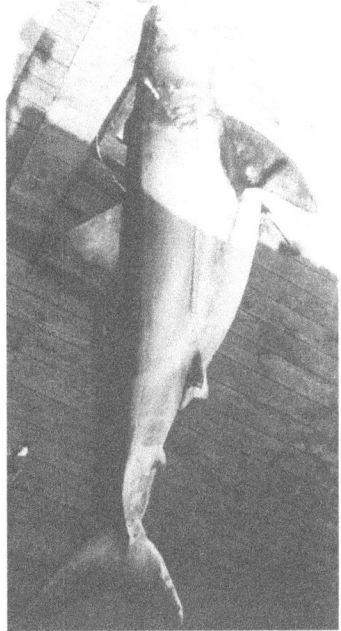

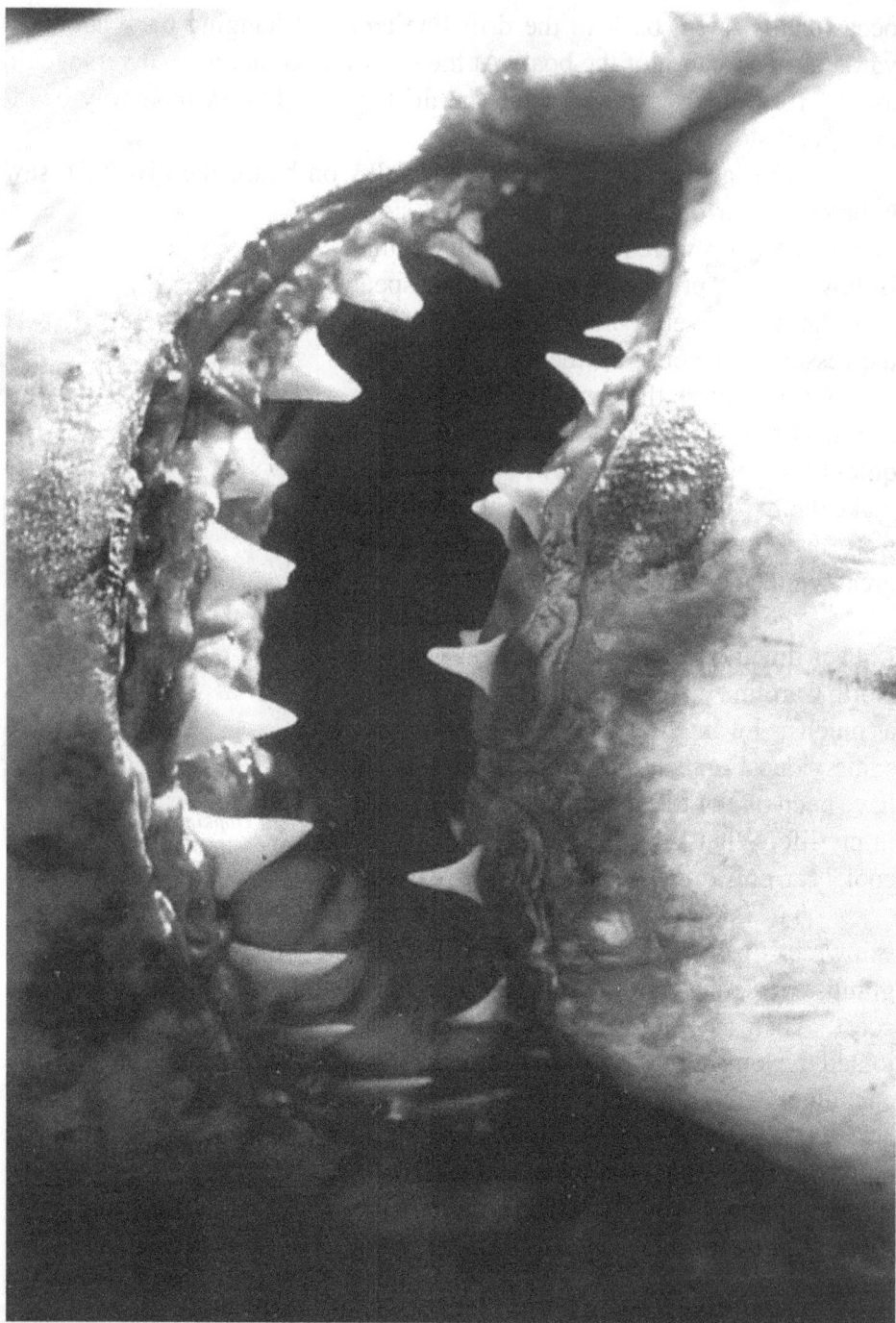

The rows of large teeth in the mouth of Glen Hopkins' great white chilled spectators when it was hauled onto the docks at Ocracoke. (Photo: Jim Francesconi, N.C. Div. of Marine Fisheries)

5
GREAT WHITES FROM
BOGUE BANKS TO CAPE FEAR

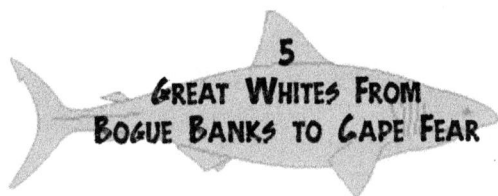

Along the North Carolina coast from Bogue Banks on the north to Cape Fear in the south, the coastline makes a large arc. The ocean contained within this arc is known as Onslow Bay. On the west end of the Bogue Banks is Bogue Inlet, the spot where, if you are traveling south down the coast, the Outer Banks officially end. The White Oak River flows past the historic town of Swansboro and into the Atlantic Ocean via this inlet. To the east, on the Bogue Banks, is Emerald Isle, while on the west is Bear Island and Hammocks Beach State Park.

On March 29th, 1986, a great white shark was caught in Bogue Inlet. The shark measured 12 feet long. "It was caught right in the inlet, near buoy 8 or 9," says Dr. Schwartz. "Sportsmen most likely caught it." Other than this, not much is known about this shark.

A month later and about 20 miles further offshore, another great white was landed in this area. This one was quite a large catch, measuring 15 feet 9 inches long, and weighing 2143 pounds. Not much is known about the circumstances surrounding the capture of this shark. Some long-line fishermen working out of Morehead City took it. This is the largest great white shark accurately measured and independently verified to be taken along the North Carolina coast in the late twentieth century, barely exceeding the great white landed by Lloyd Davidson and company a year and a half earlier.

One of the largest sharks ever encountered off the Bogue Banks, or anywhere else for that matter, was seen back in 1988. Tony Austin, a commercial fisherman who lived on Harker's Island, was fishing for grouper with a friend one night about 20 miles off Emerald Isle.

Measuring 14 feet 7 inches, this great white shark was found in the Intracoastal Waterway near Wilmington, N.C. on December 12, 1998. (Photo: Bill Parker, N.C. Aquarium at Fort Fisher)

As he stood along the side of the boat, in the stern of the vessel, he looked over into the ocean and noticed part of an enormous fin sticking out of the water. "I could have reached over and touched it," Austin later recalled.

His friend, who was standing in the very front of the vessel, saw the shark at the very same moment Austin called out to him to take a look at the large shark. They observed what is without a doubt one of the largest great whites ever seen in the wild.

"I was in the stern and the other guy was in the front of the boat," said Austin. "I saw the tail and my friend simultaneously saw the head." Since their fishing boat was 26 feet long, and the shark was approximately the same size as their vessel, Austin is sure that the shark that visited his boat that evening was approximately 26 feet long.

The shark stayed with them for a few minutes, grabbing the lead fishing weight that was dangling in the water and spitting it out. The shark then departed. During the entire episode, the shark did not exhibit any aggressive behavior.

Austin is an experienced mariner who has had many adventures on the oceans, and has seen all kinds of sharks. He has no doubt about what he saw that evening, especially his calculations concerning the shark's size relative to the boat. He was also positive that the shark in question was a great white.

Before he started telling people about his encounter, Austin realized it would be nice to have some way to back up his tale. He thus set about establishing the shark's identity beyond the shadow of a doubt. He remembered the lead weights the shark had twice taken into its mouth that evening, and upon closer inspection found some bite marks and tooth fragments. With these, he realized, the shark could be positively identified.

The fragments were taken to Dr. Schwartz over in Morehead City. Based on these fragments, Dr. Schwartz confirmed that Austin's visitor that evening off the Bogue Banks was indeed a great white shark.

Further south along Onslow Bay, the waters off Cape Fear are frequented by several different species of large sharks. Whale sharks, basking sharks, tiger sharks, thresher sharks and several varieties of hammerhead have all been seen or caught in the area. There have also been encounters with great whites.

"We have white sharks here, and they are usually here in the winter," observed Bill Parker of the North Carolina Aquarium at Fort Fisher. "Because we don't have the huge seal population, they are more likely to be chasing

This great white was caught two miles off Wrightsville Beach by Dean Jordan, Hubert Jordan, and Danny Sullivan in 1985. (Photo: Don Hammond, S.C. Dept. of Natural Resources)

squid schools. They are more likely to be found in quite a bit deeper water like the Steeples, where it's over 300 feet deep or more."

On rare occasions, great whites have been observed close to the beaches along the Cape Fear coast. On April 27th, 1985, a great white was caught two miles off Wrightsville Beach, roughly a mile north of the Wrightsville Jetty. Dean Jordan, Hubert Jordan and William Sullivan, were on a fishing trip working the waters between Cape Fear and Winyah Bay. They landed several sharks, including a large tiger shark, but the most interesting fish was a large shark they believed to be a great white. This fish was an immature female that measured 7 feet 8 inches long and weighed 250 pounds.

Since none of the three fishermen had ever seen a great white in person before, they were not certain about the identity of the shark. So upon returning to their home port of Georgetown, South Carolina, they contacted the South Carolina Department of Natural Resources to get help identifying the fish. Don Hammond, a fisheries biologist with the department, investigated the shark and positively identified it as a great white.

Another instance of someone spotting a great white near shore occurred back on May 18th, 1996, when two passengers aboard a 10' boat encountered an enormous great white just off Wrightsville Beach. The people who were on board the small craft believed the shark to be approximately 20 feet long. They were sure it was a great white, as they got a good look at the shark's distinctive teeth. The great white made what the couple perceived to be a few threatening gestures, which prompted them to leave the area with much haste.

There was another report of a large great white in the area that very same day. According to Dr. Schwartz, this one was spotted by some divers who were moored off the Testing Buoy near 5 Mile Reef. Whether or not this was the same great white as the one encountered by the small craft closer to Wrightsville Beach is unknown.

Not all encounters with great whites along the Cape Fear coast have occurred in the ocean. Remarkably, on at least two occasions, great whites have been spotted in inshore waters near the mouth of the Cape Fear.

In the summer of 1998, John Woods III was fishing from his 19 1/2-foot boat in the main channel of the Cape Fear River between Bald Head Island and Southport . He caught three small sharks ranging in size from a foot to a foot-and-a-half long. Much blood was spilt as he was attempting to release the third shark, and as Woods leaned over the side of his boat to wash his hands, he noticed that he was not alone.

"I looked down into the water and less than a foot away from my bloody hands was an eyeball the size of a saucer looking back at me," said Woods. "I did see the gray tops and sides and the tell-tale white bottom as he passed the boat at a 45 degree angle. He must have come up behind the boat to avoid hitting it. His tail came slightly out of the water before he went back down, and I left the area! His eye was 4 and half to five inches across."

By Woods' reckoning, this was an enormous great white. "I watched the animal's front end pass the front of my boat (19 1/2 feet). Then I looked back and I could see its tail...still four feet beyond the back of my boat. This animal had to be between 25 and 30 feet in length."

Later that same year another great white was spotted in the inshore waters near Cape Fear. This

Bill Parker examines the remains of the white shark found in the Intracoastal Waterway. (Photo: Bill Parker, N.C. Aquarium at Fort Fisher)

one was found floating dead on the water by some fishermen in the Intracoastal Waterway near Wilmington on December 12th, 1998. They reported their find to the Wrightsville Coast Guard Station. Fifteen Coast Guardsmen hauled the massive shark out of the water near the end of Bozeman Road, not far from channel marker 154 between Masonboro Island and the mainland. Parker was called in from the aquarium at Fort Fisher to have a look at this large shark.

"We had a 14 foot 7 inch long total length female white shark," said Parker. "It was very large, 9 feet in girth around the pectorals. Her mouth was large enough to have bitten me in half if necessary. Once I opened her up she could have swallowed me whole. She was full of squid, and was not in chasing mammals, or anything of that nature, or even larger fish."

Upon investigation, Parker found that the shark had liver damage. He suspects that the shark was shot after having raided someone's tuna catch.

Seeing this great white was a rare treat for Parker, who spends much of his time researching the various shark species that prowl the shores of southeastern North Carolina. "This is the only great white I have encountered," he noted. "It's the largest one that has been landed along the North Carolina coast since 1986."

The presence of these great whites in the Cape Fear raises several interesting questions. What compels these large sharks to leave the ocean for the shallow waters of the Cape Fear coast? Was this a freak occurrence, or do great whites frequent the mouth of the Cape Fear River, and roam along the Intracoastal Waterway? More investigation is definitely needed before these mysteries can be solved.

On April 29, 1989 Capt. Harold Olsen and the crew of the Bonzai caught this 15-foot female great white off Bulls Bay. It is the largest great white shark landed in South Carolina waters to date. (Photo: Don Hammond, S.C. Dept. of Natural Resources)

6
SOUTH CAROLINA
GREAT WHITES

On January 2nd, 2004, Mark Beasenburg and Danny Mixon were fishing for sea bass in the Atlantic Ocean approximately a dozen miles off the coast of Charleston, South Carolina. The weather was clear and the seas were calm as the two men fished from Beasenburg's 24-foot Boston Whaler.

Around 4 o'clock in the afternoon, they spied a large fin sticking out of the water less than a hundred yards from their boat, slowly but steadily swimming in their direction. At first glance, they thought their visitor was a large sunfish. Then they noticed what they thought was a fin from another sunfish several feet from the first. But as the fins got closer, the two men realized that these objects were attached to the same animal.

Beasenburg is an experienced mariner who has spent much time on the water. In addition, he is an experienced diver, and has had many encounters with a wide variety of marine life. He quickly surmised that what he was looking at was not two separate animals, but instead was the dorsal fin and tail of a large shark, possibly a whale shark or a basking shark. But as the shark passed their vessel, it became clear that this was no gentle basking or whale shark. Instead, they were looking at an enormous great white.

"As it got closer to us you could see its diamond-shaped head," said Beasenburg. "It was swimming right on top of the water, its dorsal fin and tail sticking 2 - 3 feet out of the water. As it passed us about 8 to 10 feet off the starboard side, it banked on its side and dove out of view. As it did, we saw the solid white belly."

This is the largest great white reported off the South Carolina coast since the early 1800's. Beasenburg estimates the shark to have been in excess of 20 feet long. "When it was alongside us, we could tell it was about the same size as my boat, which is a 24-footer. I estimate the shark was at least 23 feet long, maybe more."

The two men scanned the water looking to see if they could catch another glimpse of the amazing shark. Shortly, they saw it approaching their boat from behind. "We saw his fin coming up behind the boat about 30 feet away," noted Beasenburg. "He was coming in at a pretty good clip, about four or five knots."

The men stood at the back of the boat, anxiously watching the monstrous shark take aim at their vessel. The shark closed on the drifting boat, finally stopping its charge when less than a foot away. The great white maintained its position with its nose approximately 3 inches away from the twin 150 horsepower Johnson engines.

"This thing stopped about 3 inches off our props," said Beasenburg. "It just hung there for several seconds, looking us over. He was so close I could have reached over the transom and touched his nose. Because he was so big and in so close, I could only see one eye on his head, and my buddy who was standing on the opposite side of the boat, could only see the other eye from where he was standing. It was so close not only could I see the big black eye, but I could see the jelly-like substance around the eye."

After staring at the huge shark for several seconds, Beasenburg dashed off to get his camera. But before he found it, the shark swam away.

When they returned to port, the two men reported their encounter to the U.S. Coast Guard. So far, there have been no other confirmed sightings of their great white off the South Carolina coast. However, Beasenburg later learned that there were reports of a large shark, possibly a great white, feeding on a whale carcass in the vicinity of where he and Mixon sighted their great white.

In South Carolina, fishermen working offshore occasionally catch great whites. So far, the earliest known documented encounter with one of these large fish only dates back to the mid-20th century. This is unusual, considering South Carolina's long maritime tradition, and it is quite possible that encounters occurred down through the centuries that have not been written down and have long since been forgotten.

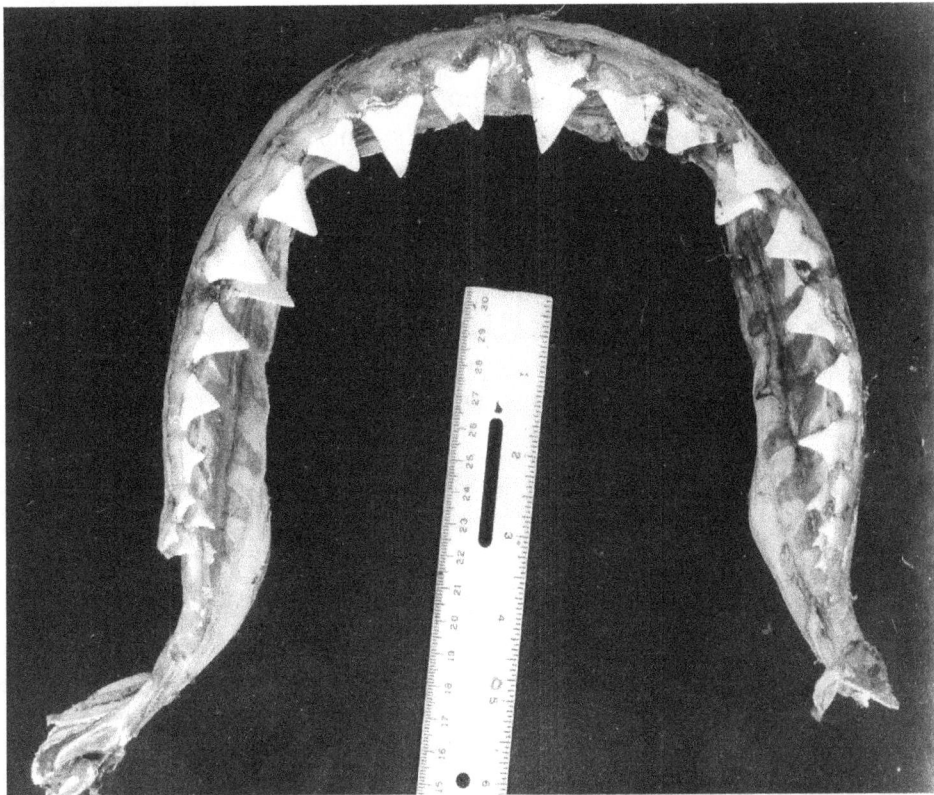

Part of a great white jaw from the shark caught by R.T. Morrison off Cape Romain, S.C. in April 1950. (Photo: Charleston Museum)

The two exceptions to this were perhaps the two 25-foot long sharks encountered off Charleston back in the 1800's. As noted earlier, Captain Ferguson of Charleston related that two 25 foot long sharks were seen on two separate occasions between 1835 and 1840, the former was captured and the latter killed a man in Charleston Harbor. Detailed descriptions of these sharks is non-existent, yet based on the sharks' size, it is probable that they were great whites.

Over a century passed before the first verified specimen of a great white shark was caught off South Carolina. Back in the spring of 1950, fishermen working off the South Carolina coast reported catching a number of great whites. Charles Bearden, a scientist who researched the sharks in these waters back in the mid 20th century, made a brief note of these catches. "No records of the white shark for South Carolina were found in the literature," he wrote, "but E. Milby Burton of the Charleston Museum recorded several specimens which were taken by trawlers off Cape Romain in April and May of 1950."

R.T. Morrison, Jr., was on one of these fishing trawlers off the South Carolina coast that landed a great white in April of 1950 . The shark, which measured 12 1/2 feet long, was taken off Cape Romain. Morrison later donated the set of jaws from his shark to the Charleston Museum.

Between 1959 and 1961, two reported encounters with a great white in the nearshore waters of South Carolina were reported. The first occurred September 26th, 1959, when three Marines were fishing in the waters of Albergotti Creek near Beaufort. Just before midnight, the men saw a large shark thrashing about in the waters nearby. The shark turned its attention on the fishermen, ramming their boat over and over. How they were able to identify the shark is unclear, but they maintained it was, "a man-eating white shark."

Two years later, on August 16th, 1961, a young man was attacked and wounded by what witnesses claimed was a great white shark in the waters off Pawley's Island. These incidents, which will be discussed later in this book, are among the rare episodes of a great white shark attack documented off the southeastern United States in the 20th century.

Nearly a quarter century passed before another great white was documented along the South Carolina coast. In 1984, a great white was landed off Cape Romain. This was the second time this particular shark had been caught. In 1981, it was hooked over 500 miles to the north, off the coast of Long Island, New York. Fishermen cooperating with scientists from the Cooperative Shark Tagging Program tagged the shark and then released it. This was the first tagged and released great white marked in this program to be recaptured .

Midway between Charleston and Myrtle Beach, Winyah Bay forms an opening along the South Carolina coast where the waters of the Pee Dee River and its tributaries flow into the Atlantic. For many years, ships bearing indigo, rice, cotton and other commodities have traversed this bay on their way to and from Georgetown. Two rock jetties reach out into the ocean at the mouth of the bay, providing a relatively safe shipping channel. These rock jetties are also a popular place where recreational fishermen target the various species of fish that thrive here on this man made rock wall.

On July 11th, 1987, the DeMaurice family of Darlington was fishing the waters off these jetties when they had an encounter with a shark they are not likely to forget. The weather was fair and the seas were smooth as R. W. "Bubba" DeMaurice motored his 17 foot boat across Winyah Bay from the boating access south of Georgetown to the jetties. Three generations of the DeMaurice family were along for the trip, including his father, Billy, daughter B.J. and wife June.

As they moved into a spot adjacent to one of the jetties, Bubba stopped the boat and his wife let the anchor drop into the water. Before the anchor could make its way to the bottom, something really big seized it. At first, Bubba did not realize what was going on, but the actions of his wife and daughter, along with their exclamations of, "He's got it in his mouth!" let him know that something was wrong. As he looked over the edge of the boat, he saw that the line holding the anchor was being dragged through the water, and then went slack as whatever had taken the anchor was headed for the surface. An instant later, an enormous shark erupted from below as it thrashed about on the surface of the water just a few feet from their boat.

"The anchor was lodged in the side of his mouth as he came up," recalled June. "I still remember it as if it were yesterday and I still have a hard time being on a small boat. The shark's mouth was large enough that I could fit my entire head and shoulders down its mouth. It came up at the bow of the boat, mouth open, extended back with many teeth showing. As it was hooked on the anchor, it extended outwards a time or two, and it appeared to be the length of the boat. There were no stripes on this shark. It was not a tiger shark. It was not a mako. I'm sure of that."

Based on her observations of the shark while it was stretched out on the surface and as she was staring into its mouth, June concluded that the shark she was looking at was a great white. The head was triangular shaped, not pointed like a mako nor rounded like a bull shark. The teeth were large and triangular in shape, not curved like a tiger shark nor small and conical shaped like a basking shark. In addition, the shark was colored a dark grey on top, and was lighter underneath.

Mr. DeMaurice did not get a good enough look at the shark to make a positive identification. "I have no idea what kind it was," he recalled. "I do remember the tail as being symmetrical and the length in the 12 foot range. I never got a good look at his head. My wife and little girl were the only ones that saw the head when they pulled the anchor out and he first picked up."

Unable to shake free of the anchor, the shark went back underwater, dragging the front of the boat under the surface for a brief moment, then whipping the boat about in the water. The shark headed back up toward the surface and started swimming for the deeper waters of the ocean.

Bubba DeMaurice realized the boat was being pulled out into the Atlantic, and something drastic had to be done before the shark reached the deep waters, where it would possibly swamp the vessel. He kept a cool head as he sized up the situation. Instead of struggling with the shark and risk swamping his boat, he let the fish pull them out towards the ocean while his wife tried cutting the rope with what must have seemed a ridiculously inadequate filet knife. After about thirty seconds of vigorously hewing at the rope, she successfully severed the line. The shark headed out to sea, and the DeMaurice family headed for shore.

Whether or not the shark was able to free itself from the anchor is unknown. As to what possessed the large fish to grab their anchor in the first place, Bubba DeMaurice has a theory. "I think the shark probably mistakenly thought the anchor was a skate when it entered the water as skates were plentiful and he was probably feeding on them."

Without question, the person who has had the most encounters with great white sharks off the South Carolina coast is Captain Harold Olsen. He has been fishing for sharks in these waters for more than twenty-five years from his 42' sharkfishing boat called the *Bonzai*, and during his time on the water he has seen and caught numerous white sharks.

"I've caught at least two or three a year for the past twenty-five years," says Olsen. "It would have been more than that if we had been looking specifically for these kind of fish, as we would have been using heavier gear. But we're generally fishing for much smaller sharks, so the really big great whites have no trouble breaking our lines."

Olsen points out that the white sharks he has caught have been of all manner of sizes, both large and small. Some of the smaller ones were approximately four feet long, while the largest has been over fifteen feet.

"I normally catch them in the wintertime, and the majority have been caught in January and February" notes Olsen. "I fish for smooth dogfish in 58° degree water, and great whites will go down the line eating sharks we've hooked, swallowing four-foot sharks whole. I had one come up around the boat one day that had a four-foot shark in its mouth. As it swam around our boat, it just kept carrying the smaller shark around in its mouth like a dog carrying a bone."

A close up view of the great white shark caught by Capt. Harold Olsen and the crew of the Bonzai in April 1989 off Bulls Bay, S.C. (Photo: Don Hammond, S.C. Dept. of Natural Resources)

Amazingly, the largest sharks he deals with are not white sharks, but are instead tiger sharks. He has caught several large tiger sharks weighing more than 2,000 pounds which were much larger than any great white he has landed. "These are some dark and deadly waters off Charleston." says Olsen. "It's not really the great whites you have to worry about, though. These waters are full of bull sharks and lemon sharks close inshore, tiger sharks a little farther out."

With all of this time spent on the water looking for sharks, it is no wonder that Olsen is credited with landing the largest great white ever taken in South Carolina waters. On April 26th, 1989, he and his crewmates were fishing in 21 fathoms of water several miles off Bulls Bay when they landed the huge fish. Although most large white sharks are usually caught by becoming tangled in fishing gear, this particular one was actually hooked in the corner of its mouth, unable to bite through the leader and escape.

The shark was too large to hoist on board the *Bonzai*, so it was secured to a rope and towed back into port. On the way in, Olsen alerted the wildlife officials in Charleston that he was bringing in a great white shark, but they had a hard time believing the veracity of the tale. "Right when I was coming through the harbor, I called the wildlife department and told them we had a great white," recalled Olsen. "They didn't believe me at first, and must have asked me ten times, 'Are you sure it's a great white?' Once they realized I was serious, they decided to come out and take a look. As they were coming up behind us, the shark rolled over where they could get a good look at its belly, and they hollered out, 'It is a great white!'"

The fishermen returned to Shem Creek, where the great white was hauled out for everyone to see. People from all around the Charleston area made their way down to the dock to get a good look at the huge fish.

"It was a 15 feet total length female great white," recalled marine biologist Don Hammond, who was called in to examine the shark's remains. "She weighed 1,231.1 pounds, and had a half girth of 40 inches."

Captain Olsen landed another great white less than a month later, while fishing much closer to shore. This shark, which measured a mere seven feet long, was caught just off the entrance to Charleston Harbor.

Ironically, Olsen was not the only person encountering great white sharks in these waters back in the spring of 1989. Todd Smith, a student from the College of Charleston, and a friend were snorkeling approximately 200 yards off the Isle of Palms when they were pulled from the water by the U.S. Coast Guard. One of his rescuers informed Smith that they were swimming in waters where a white shark had been spotted, and told them not to go back into the water. They also learned that a shark, "at least 22 feet long," had been seen in Shem Creek on at least two occasions in the preceding weeks. Was this really a great white shark, and if so, what was the reason for this large shark being so close inshore? No one will ever know for sure.

One of the most remarkable catches of a great white along the South Carolina coast occurred on December 15th, 1995. Rick Stringer, a devoted recreational shark fisherman, was fishing about five miles off Folly Beach when he hooked a large shark that he reeled in after a 15 minute fight. He grabbed the leader and prepared to tag what he thought was a dusky shark, but as soon as Stringer got a good look at the fish, he realized he had hooked a seven-foot long great white.

"The pointed snout, black eyes and large gill slits, together with the unmistakable teeth, made identification immediate and absolute," recalled Stringer. "It was an immature male with a large bite mark on its flank. Above, its color was light bronze, while below was snow white."

Instead of bringing the shark back to shore, Stringer decided to tag it and let it go. Had he brought it in, it is certain that he would have set a South Carolina recreational fishing record for a great white caught with a rod and reel. But the fisherman felt it was more important to let the rare shark return to the deep than to bring home its remains as a trophy.

Stringer is an authority on sharks in the Charleston area, having caught over 1,500 sharks in the waters off Folly Beach since 1967. Most of these sharks he has measured, studied, tagged and then released back into the wild. The great white he hooked off Folly Beach in 1995 is the only one he has actually landed, though he had an encounter with what he feels certain was another great white a few years later.

"I was using a live clear-nose skate as bait, and something took a bite out of its wings," he said. "The bite radius proved that it had to be a great white, as they are the only sharks feeding out there that time of year in 55 degree water that could have inflicted such a bite."

The most famous great white taken along the South Carolina coast is on display at Coastal Carolina University, near Conway. This shark is notable for its size, but it's not the fish's gargantuan proportions that are of note. Instead, this great white is known for its smallness.

In July of 1993, Steve Shelley, captain of the fishing boat *Molly D* out of Little River, South Carolina, was long-lining about 50 miles off the coast of Charleston. As the line was pulled in, a crewman noticed that a shark had somehow gotten tangled in the line and had died. Once the fish was aboard, they realized it was a great white.

Upon closer inspection, they found that their great white was very young. The shark weighed only 29 pounds, and measured 51 1/2 inches long. It still had the protective sheath over its teeth, which protects the mother great white from receiving potentially dreadful wounds while giving birth.

"Without question, this is the youngest great white caught in these waters," says Hammond, who came up from Charleston to Little River to investigate the shark. "The umbilical scar was prominent, and the fleshy sheath was still covering the shark's teeth."

Shelley and his crew hoped their catch would set a record for the smallest great white ever taken, as there was a rather substantial monetary reward being offered for such a catch. However, they were not successful. Their catch was just a shade bigger than a 48-inch great white reeled in by a New York fisherman back in 1983.

The presence of this pup raises an interesting question. Do great whites regularly give birth to their pups off the coast of North and South

Capt. Steve Shelley holds "Baby Jaws," the great white shark he caught off the S.C. coast in July 1993. (Photo: Don Hammond, S.C. Dept. of Natural Resources)

Carolina? In addition to the shark landed by Shelley, other juvenile great whites have been found along the Carolina coast. Dr. Schwartz has documented other great whites that were less than 5 feet long. In July of 1983 a 4 foot 5 1/2 inch specimen was taken by a surf fisherman on the western end of Onslow Beach, which is located within the bounds of Camp Lejeune Marine Base. On December 13th, 1984, a 4 foot 8 1/4-inch great white was caught near the *Papoose* shipwreck not too far from Cape Lookout. In May of 1996, three great white pups were found at Ocracoke.

In addition to these specimens that were actually captured, there have been instances of divers reporting what they believed were young great whites swimming with a larger shark. This was reported from the great whites encountered off Cape Lookout in 2000 and 2001.

Despite the presence of these very young sharks, there is no concrete, independently verified proof that great whites use the waters off North and South Carolina as pupping grounds. Scientists are at a loss to explain exactly where great whites normally go to give birth in the North Atlantic. Many believe that the large fish give birth to their young at scattered locations along the edge of the continental shelf.

"Nobody really knows, because nobody has ever seen a pregnant great white in the western North Atlantic," explains Dr. Jose Castro, a shark expert from the National Marine Fisheries Service in Miami, Florida. Dr. Castro has spent many years studying the pupping grounds used by the various species of sharks off the southeastern United States, and he has never found any evidence of great whites using the area for such a purpose. "I surmise that they are giving birth in the same area as mako sharks, out in the ocean from the Sargasso Sea south to the Lesser Antilles."

Word of the young great white caught by Shelley off the South Carolina coast spread far and wide, and soon museums and marine biologists expressed an interest in acquiring the shark. Somewhere along the line, it was given the name "Baby Jaws." But the shark lost much of its appeal to the various museums as the news spread that it was not small enough to be a record setting fish. Soon, interest in the shark waned.

One individual who remained interested in this shark was Glenn Reed, owner of an attraction in Myrtle Beach known as Shark's Tooth Cove. The museum had several artifacts from a variety of sharks, including fossils from sharks that had long since died. Reed contacted Shelley about acquiring Baby Jaws for his collection.

"It had no monetary value but the educational value is priceless," recalled Reed. Soon a deal was struck, and Reed had a friend who was also a taxidermist make a mount of the shark for Shelley. The actual remains of the shark then went to Reed. After many trials and tribulations, Baby Jaws went on display at Shark's Tooth Cove. Reed assembled a 40-gallon tank filled with denatured alcohol to preserve and display the rare great white.

Baby Jaws became quite a tourist attraction. Crowds thronged Reed's museum to catch a glimpse of the great white that had been caught off the South Carolina coast. People from all over the world dropped by Shark's Tooth Cove to take a look at this rare shark. Among the notable visitors was Rodney Fox, the Australian who survived an attack by a great white and is now one of the world's foremost experts on these sharks.

"Baby Jaws" now rests in a special tank designed by Glenn Reid, who donated it to Coastal Carolina University in Conway, S.C.

"Even Rodney was blown away when he saw Baby Jaws," recalled Reed. "He just could not believe that this killer creature starts out as small as it looked and is defenseless. The teeth in this shark were maybe a half-inch to three-quarters at the most. When we first thawed Baby Jaws I noticed that the teeth were translucent, much like the feet of a horse when they are first born, before they solidify."

Upon closing his museum, Reed generously donated Baby Jaws and the display tank to Coastal Carolina University in nearby Conway. The shark was given with the understanding that it was not to be dissected or cut up for experiments.

"This was the only known baby great white that was still intact," said Reed. "The other two that we know of were all cut up and processed for research projects. To our knowledge this is the only one that has been preserved."

After nearly a decade, the shark's remains continue to rest in the 40-gallon tank of denatured alcohol that Reed built. The display now resides on the second floor of the Marine Biology Department at Coastal Carolina.

The year 2008 has brought several reports of white sharks from the waters off South Carolina. In April, Charles Stone and Lee Elkins took Stone's two grandsons, Austin and Taylor, fishing in the Atlantic. They headed southeast from Murrells Inlet, heading for the site of the shipwreck of the *Vermillion*, whose remains lie on the bottom of the ocean over a hundred feet deep. This is normally a good spot to fish for snappers, sea bass and grouper. On this occasion, they were catching amberjack. Stone described the weather as, "beautiful," with a water temperature of 68°, calm seas and good visibility under the water.

While drift fishing over the wreck, they looked down into the water and saw what they thought was a large tiger shark circling the school of amberjack they were trying to catch. As the shark came closer to the surface and passed by their 27' long vessel, the elder Stone realized that the large shark was no tiger shark, and unlike any shark he had ever seen before in his thirty years of fishing in these waters. Mr. Stone is not only an experienced angler, but he is the owner of the Marlin Quay Marina at Murrells Inlet, so he has seen his share of the local fish species down through the years, including all manner of sharks that live in South Carolina waters.

"There is no question in my mind that this was anything other than a great white," says Mr. Stone. "On his closest pass, he came up the port side

This great white was captured and released May 3, 2008 near Garden City, S.C., by researchers from Ripley's Believe It or Not Aquarium at Myrtle Beach.
(Photo: Joe Choromanski ©2008 Ripley Entertainment, Inc.)

of the boat, turned and swam by the stern of the boat, made a turn, went down deeper into the water and swam away. He was not more than two feet from our boat. I've seen many different kinds of fish, and caught all kinds of sharks: bull sharks, tiger sharks, makos, hammerheads. This was clearly not one of them. All of us who were there agree that it was a great white."

Though he is quite certain as to the shark's identity, Mr. Stone could only offer an estimate of the shark's size. Not wishing to seem outlandish, he is conservative with his estimate of the shark's length, and places it at approximately 15 feet. He bases this on the size of the shark in relation to the length of his boat, but and would rather underestimate than overestimate the massive shark's size.

Two weeks later, on May 3rd, 2008, just offshore from the world famous Grand Strand beaches, Joe Choramanski and fellow researchers from the Ripley's Believe it or Not® Aquarium at Myrtle Beach were catching sharks for research purposes related to the aquarium. On this day, instead of a bull or blacktip shark, they found a great white shark on their line. The fish was caught in 34 feet of water approximately five miles off Garden City, South Carolina. The shark was a female, and measured 10 feet long. The water temperature was 68.5° F.

The researchers theorize that the shark was attracted to the vicinity of where they were working by the remains of a whale or other dead mammal. They noticed some sort of oily slick on the surface of the water, and theorized that the animal's remains were under the surface of the sea.

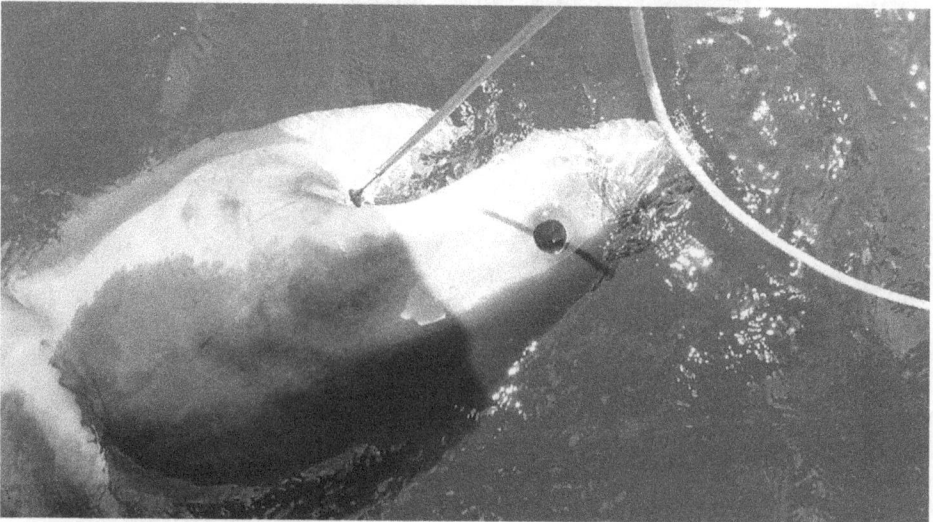

The Garden City great white captured and released by Ripley's Believe It or Not Aquarium researchers. (Photo: Joe Choromanski ©2008 Ripley Entertainment, Inc.)

Bystanders were startled to see this great white shark washed up on the beach near Morris Island Lighthouse in S.C.

After measurements, the shark was tagged with a National Marine Fisheries Service Apex Predator tag and then released. The shark was in good condition when it was let go back into the ocean, and it is hoped that it survived the ordeal. With any luck, at some point in the future, the shark's tag will be retrieved and the fish's movements can be followed, which will do much to shed more light on the movements of great white sharks along the coast of the southeastern United States.

The last great white of the year reported from South Carolina was found on November 18th, 2008, stranded in shallow water near the Morris Island Lighthouse on the south side of the entrance to Charleston Harbor. A beachcomber discovered the shark, and reported it to the S.C. Department of Natural Resources. Jon Geddings and Josh Loefer were dispatched to examine the shark, which was found to be a female great white measuring 13 feet two inches long total length. Preliminary examination showed no signs of diseases, nor any indication that the fish was sick.

Exactly why and how this large shark came to be on the beach in Charleston will remain a mystery. The shark showed no visible signs of trauma, and scientists can only guess as to how it came to rest here on Morris Island. If the shark had been caught inadvertently offshore, released and then died from the trauma, it must have been caught not too far away, as there were no signs that predators, including other sharks, had been feeding on the great white's carcass. A more likely possibility is that as the shark was swimming in the waters off Morris Island, she was caught in shallow water and stranded on the sandy beach by the falling tide. Unlike marine mammals such as dolphins which breath oxygen and can survive a few hours when they are stranded out of the water, a stranded shark would soon perish after being stranded on a beach out of the water, and is unlikely to survive long enough to be freed by a rising tide.

Great white sharks have been seen and encountered off South Carolina for many years, and will undoubtedly continue showing up here for many years to come. Much remains to be learned about these amazing fish off the coast of the Palmetto State.

7
GEORGIA GREAT WHITES

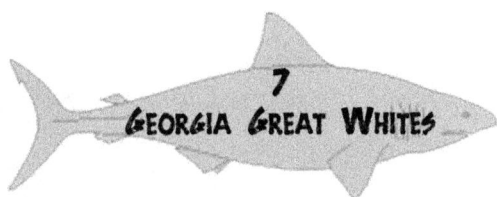

Great whites are the subjects of many tall tales and legends. Occasionally there are reports of some truly monstrous specimens being caught or observed. One huge shark, estimated to be somewhere between 22 and 25 feet long, was seen in March of 2000 by a group of people fishing off the Georgia coast. Fortunately, they brought back photos to back up their fish story.

Chris Curry, his wife and three friends—Eric Adamski, Eddie Joslyn and Jeremy Merklinger, watched the fish as it passed underneath Curry's 26' fishing boat called the *Catillac* as it was anchored off St. Catherine's Island, about 30 miles south of Fort McAllister and the mouth of the Savannah River. They were fishing for seabass in 80 feet of water over a landmark known as the Anchor Ledge. The sea was very flat, and the water temperature was approximately 55° F.

Earlier in the day, they had hits from a few really big fish, including a large shark. One shark in particular they managed to get within 20 feet of the boat before it broke the line. Adamski estimated this shark to have been approximately 14 feet long. "Looked like a great white," says Adamski, "but I didn't think that's what it was because they aren't usually seen in the Savannah area."

About thirty minutes after the 14-footer got away, the group saw the biggest fish any of them had ever seen in their lives. As he was standing on the starboard side of the boat trying to help Joslyn with an equipment problem, Chris Curry looked over the edge of the boat and saw something large moving

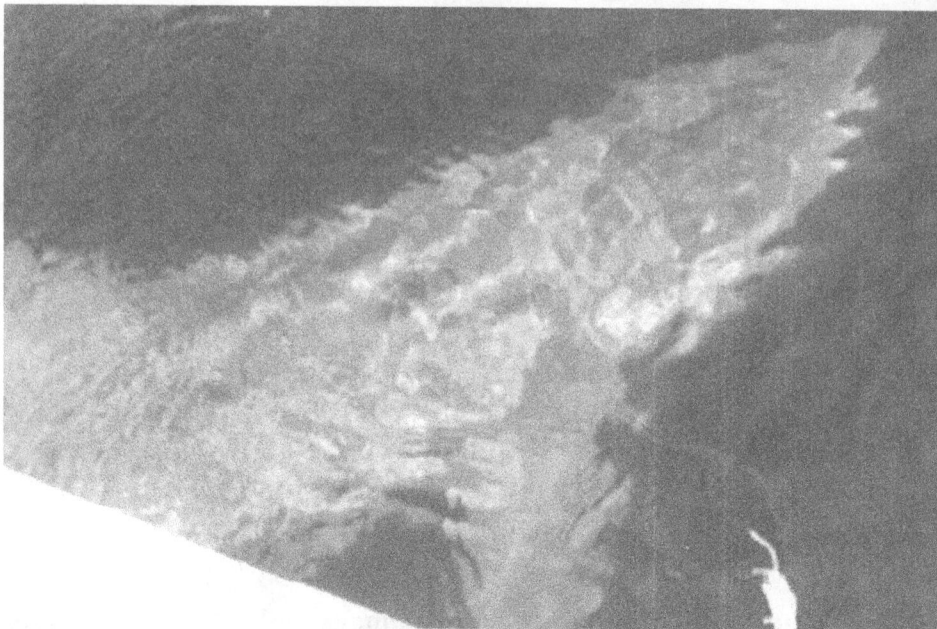

Eric Adamski captured this shot of a great white that visited the boat Catillac *off the Georgia coast in March 2000. (Photo: Eric Adamski)*

up out of the depths toward their vessel. As the shark neared the surface, it passed slowly along the starboard side of the boat, giving all on board an up close look at a great white shark.

"I can recall it going down the side of the boat slowly," said Curry. "It wasn't acting aggressive. I did notice that it had the largest black eyes. The water was so clear I could see the ampullae on its nose. The girth of it was what was so impressive. The length of it was unbelievable but to me the girth was really large."

Adamski was standing next to Curry, and saw the shark as it was rising toward them. "Chris and I both had lines in the water. Chris had reeled in two fish right past the shark's head, and it didn't flinch or anything. It didn't even beat its tail; it just glided by very peacefully. I also had a line in the water and I had to actually move my rod tip around the shark to avoid possibly rubbing against its right pectoral fin."

Looking over the edge of the boat into the water, Joslyn was just in time to see the shark pass. He, too, was impressed with the size of the fish. "All I could think of was if this fish beats his tail one good time he's going to knock us over. I mean, he had to have been as big as the boat or bigger."

Lisa Curry looked over her husband's shoulder down into the water in time to see the shark rising toward the surface on its first pass. She clearly remembers seeing the shark's distinctive coloration of gray on top and white underneath. She was also impressed with the shark's teeth as its mouth hung slightly open.

"He was just kind of filtering water," she noted. "It was like he was trying to pick up some vibrations from the engine with his teeth."

"As the shark passed by it dropped a little deeper and banked to the left," recalled Adamski. "At that point someone yelled, 'Get the gaff!' and I said, 'Forget the gaff, we need a camera.'"

So Adamski went into the cabin, got his camera, then returned to the back of the boat where he hopped up on top of the coolers to look out for the shark. He was just in time, as their visitor was making a second run at the boat.

"I saw the shark off the port side of the boat, and I tried to take a few pictures but the gunwale was in the way. So the shark went under the boat," said Adamski. The shark passed slightly under the boat amidships from port to starboard, slightly deeper than it had been on its first run. After the shark emerged on the starboard side, Adamski was able to get an unobstructed view. "I held the button down and I got three shots."

Based on their observations, those on board the *Catillac* that day maintain that the shark was approximately 25 feet long. All agree that as the shark passed the boat on its first pass, its head was alongside the motors while its tail was near the front of the vessel. Comparing the size of the vessel, which is 26 feet long, to the size of the shark, they come to their estimates of its length. They have made a conscious effort not to exaggerate or seem outlandish, and prefer to err on the side of conservativeness.

Using a cleat attached very near to the rear of the boat, Adamski made an effort to determine how long their visitor was. "I noticed that the nose was at the back cleat, and I looked back at the bow of the boat to see the tail. It was about at the bow, but I still couldn't make out the end of it."

Chris Curry is the most conservative of the group in estimating the shark's size. He states, "From the engines to the tip of the boat is 30 feet long, with the pulpit. His tail was toward the front and his head was out the back. I've just told people he was around 22 feet. Could have been greater, could have been less, I don't really know. But it was so impressive it doesn't really matter to me, two or three feet either way.

"He didn't show a lot of aggression. But it's easy to see how something that large and known to be that powerful could create some pretty serious havoc on this size of a boat if he wished to."

On January 12, 2005 a team of whale observers captured this photo of a white shark feeding upon the remains of a right whale ten miles off the Georgia coast. (Photo: Jessica Taylor, New England Aquarium)

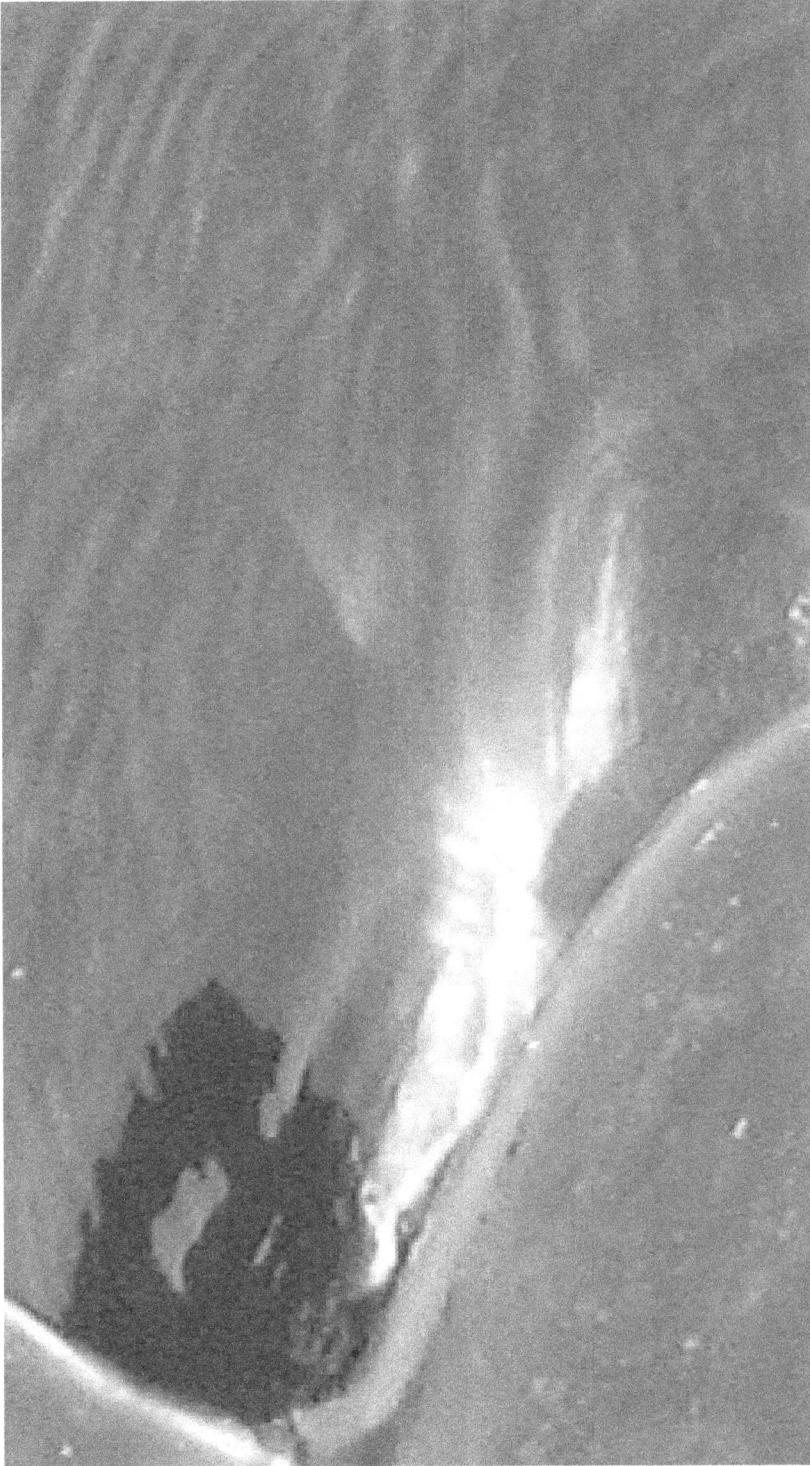

A closer view of the great white feeding off the right whale observed by whale watchers of the New England Aquarium. (Photo: Jessica Taylor)

Not all large sharks swimming in Georgia waters during the winter months are great whites, and there have been many reports of great white sightings off Georgia that have turned out to be something much less dangerous. "There have been reports by anglers that report seeing white sharks offshore," notes Henry Ansley of the Georgia Department of Natural Resources. "However, the basking shark is frequently encountered off Georgia during the winter and due to its size and similar fin configurations may account for some of these reports."

Based on their descriptions of the shark, as well as the photographs captured by Adamski, one can conclude that the shark they encountered was indeed a great white. If their calculations are correct, the giant fish that visited the *Catillac* off the coast of Georgia was one of the largest great whites ever observed in the world. Therefore this Georgia great white is truly one of the rarest of the rare.

Seeing a large great white shark like the one which visited the boat *Catillac* off Savannah in 2000 would be a rare treat anywhere in the world. But it is an especially rare event along the Georgia coast, where reports of sightings of great whites are infrequent. Although sightings of these large sharks are not reported as often as at places such as Cape Lookout, they are out there. In fact, they might be more common than people imagine.

The edge of the continental shelf is approximately 80 miles off the Georgia coastline. This is the farthest distance the edge of the shelf is from shore along the stretch of coast between Cape Hatteras and Cape Canaveral. Thus, the cooler, deeper waters the great whites prefer is well out to sea most of the year. For this reason, one could surmise that great whites are extremely unlikely visitors to the Georgia coast.

However, one thing Georgia does have to entice great whites to the area is an abundance of food, including sea turtles, fish and squid. There are also large marine mammals congregating offshore in the winter months. From November through April, the northern right whales, *Eubalaena glacialis*, gather off the Georgia and Florida coast in what is the only known northern right whale calving grounds. Dead or dying whales, as well as stray calves, make a tempting target for large great whites and other marine predators looking for a meal high in fat and caloric content.

On the morning of January 12th, 2005, a team of right whale observers from the New England Aquarium in Boston, Massachusetts, were conducting a routine right whale survey flight off the Georgia coast when they spotted the carcass of a dead whale floating on the surface of the ocean approximately 10 miles off the northern end of Cumberland Island. The two observers and their pilots spent an hour circling in an airplane 1000 feet above the whale's remains, taking photographs to document the animal for further study.

Researchers learned that the remains were those of a right whale called Lucky, an adult female that had been observed for many years off the coast of the eastern U.S.

While they were looking down upon the whale, the observers in the aircraft and the two pilots could see sharks, including at least two great whites, feeding upon the carcass. Photographs taken at the time confirmed their initial observations.

"Much of our attention at the time was focused on the dead whale," said Monica Zani, who coordinates right whale research for the New England Aquarium. "The shark was sighted by the observers a few times from the air, but they did not realize the size of the shark until later, while reviewing the images."

Zani used the size of the whale to come up with an estimate of the size of the great white. "During the necropsy of the whale's carcass, the length of the whale was 43 to 45 feet long. An adult right whale's head is approximately one third of its length. So we estimated the shark to be approximately 14-16 feet long."

The observers from the New England Aquarium were not the only ones to get a good look at the great white. Because of the scrutiny endangered northern right whales are under from scientists and conservationists who hope to save them from extinction, several individuals from various state and federal agencies converged on the scene to study the whale's remains. At least two individuals aboard a Coast Guard boat trying to secure the whale's remains and tow it ashore for research were treated to an up close visit from a white shark.

One of these individuals was Leigh Youngner of the Georgia Department of Natural Resources, who spends much of her time in the winter months keeping track of these whales. With the assistance of personnel the Coast Guard base at Brunswick, she was hoping to work with several other scientists from other government agencies, including NOAA, to study the remains and discover what caused the whale's death.

Youngner and others aboard the 47' Motor Life Boat from the Coast Guard station at Brunswick were trying to secure a line around the whale carcass and tow it back to shore, where a necropsy could be performed.

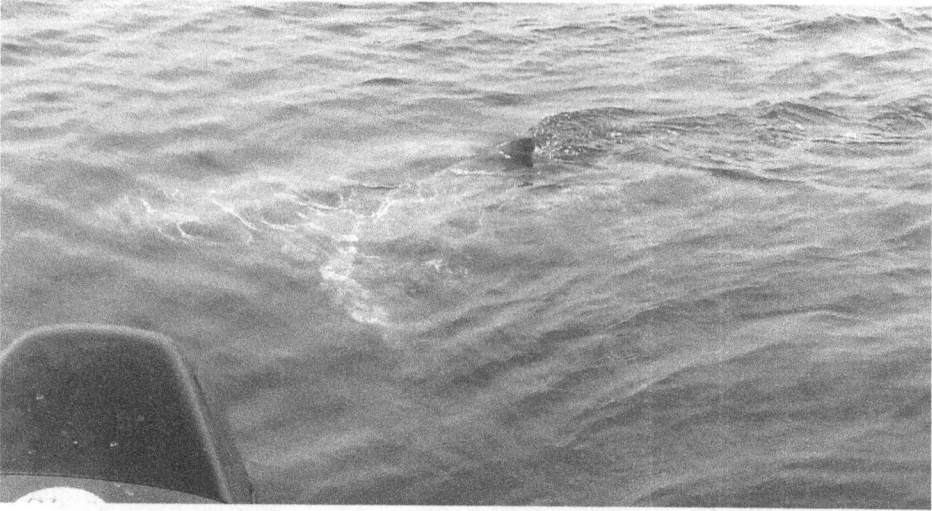

The great white shark encountered by Charles and Kathey Finney off Tybee Island, Georgia in November 2004. (Photo: Charles Finney)

Despite their best efforts, they were unsuccessful that day, and had to mark the site for a return the following day with a bigger boat.

While the researchers were trying to secure the rope, Youngner and one of the Coast Guardsmen were standing near the stern of the boat when they noticed a large shark swimming by their vessel, in the opposite direction of the dead whale. The shark passed within eight feet of where they were standing as it swam just below the surface and headed away from all the action.

As it made its pass by the boat, Youngner got a close enough look at the shark to realize it was a great white. "We knew it was a great white as soon as we saw it," she recalled. "I would estimate it was between 10 and 15 feet long."

Unable to secure the whale carcass, researchers returned to shore that evening empty-handed. The next day, they found the whale's remains had drifted off to the northwest. Several sharks of undetermined species were present feeding on the whale meat. Photos taken from the air show that there was a great white once again feeding on the large mammal.

One interesting point to ponder is how many great whites were actually present feeding on the whale. Photographs taken on both the 12th and 13th of January show a shark feeding, but it is impossible to tell if these are photos of the same shark eating on both days, or whether another had moved in to avail itself of the meal. "I believe we were all assuming it was the same shark because sightings are so rare," said Youngner. "This was such a nice meal for the shark, I don't expect that it would leave it, especially with all the competition from the other species."

Zani points out that there were at least two great whites feeding on the whale's remains on the morning of the January 12th. "According to the observers there were at least two feeding on the carcass," she says. "In one of the photographs you can see two sharks subsurface."

These photos taken by the right whale observers give photographic proof to the claims that great white sharks do indeed feed on the remains of large marine mammals off the Georgia coast. Ansley pointed out that this was the first account of a great white feeding on a whale for which there are photographs to document the episode. "It was nice to get a picture or two," he said. "We've had surface sightings before, but no photographs were taken to document them."

One of these undocumented sightings occurred seventeen years earlier when a Georgia fisherman saw a great white feeding on a whale carcass off Savannah. In the winter of 1988, charter boat Captain David Newlin encountered a great white feasting on the remains of a dead whale approximately 20 miles off the mouth of the Savannah River. He pulled his boat in close to get a good look at the shark, which was too busy eating to take much notice of its human visitors.

"I could have reached over the side of the boat and touched him," said Newlin. "That was a really big shark, a thousand pounds, minimum. Its mouth was 36 inches across."

This was not Newlin's first encounter with a great white, nor would it be his last. He recalls seeing these large sharks, "at least half-a-dozen times." His most recent sighting of a great white was in March of 2001. On that occasion, Newlin was fishing approximately 8 miles off St. Catherine's Island near the Cat Buoy when he came across a dead sea turtle floating on the surface of the ocean. He estimates the large turtle to have weighed at least 150 pounds. At the same moment, a large great white spotted the turtle as well. Newlin estimates that the shark was between 17 and 18 feet long.

The great white swam quickly to the dead turtle and consumed it with one bite. "I think he was afraid we were going to take it away from him," said Newlin, "because he just came up and swallowed that thing whole."

Newlin is not the only Savannah charter fisherman to encounter great whites in recent years. Captain Steve Amick has been fishing in these waters for 25 years. He mainly fishes for snapper in a place known as the Savannah Snapper Banks, located east of Ossabaw Island between 20 and 50 miles offshore.

This white shark was captured off Georgia in January 1994 by the crew of the Miss Debb, including Capt. Rodney Kehle, Jason Kehle, Jason Cochran and Danny O'Connell.
(Photo: Debbie Kehle)

In the spring of 2000, while fishing 30 miles off Ossabaw Island, one of Captain Amick's customers hooked a 20 pound snapper, but a great white took the fish before it could be reeled on board. "The water was cobalt blue and oil slick calm," recalled Amick. "I saw it and called out to my son, 'Look Scotty, a big shark.' It came up next to the boat, and circled us for about 20 minutes. I'm positive this was a great white. I don't know how big it was for certain, but it was at least 14 feet long."

The next year, Capt. Amick had another party out fishing, this time for seabass, in 90 feet of water about 35 miles off Tybee Island. On this occasion, a great white was actually hooked after it had eaten one of the seabass the fishing party had landed. After 30 minutes, the large shark was reeled up to the boat. Amick reckons the shark was approximately 12 feet long.

"We basically brought him right up to the boat," recalled Amick. "He was real docile, didn't thrash around or fight us in any way. We took the hook out and it just swam away."

On November 19th, 2004, Charles Finney and his wife, Kathey, were fishing from his boat *Set the Hook* when they had a memorable encounter with a great white. They were fishing for sea bass in 65 feet of water on a reef near the wreck of the tug *Matt Turecamo*, approximately 20 miles off Tybee Island.

The weather was clear, the sea calm, when at 10:30 a.m. Mrs. Finney spotted a fin from what appeared to be a large shark about 30 yards away and heading straight for their vessel. She pointed out the shark to her husband, and the couple watched as the large shark swam on the surface of the water near their boat.

"It came up to the stern and swam within a 30 to 50 yard radius of the stern," said Mr. Finney. "With my little knowledge of sharks, I believed I was looking at a great white. It was not aggressive, but very curious, swam up and hung around the boat for awhile, swimming back and forth."

During this time, Finney was able to size up his visitor. "I put it at a solid 12 feet," he observed, "My boat is 8 feet wide and it was close enough to tell that it was easily 4-6 feet longer than my boat was wide."

After a few minutes, the large shark departed. Strangely, 45 minutes later, it returned and repeated the behavior. After several more minutes of swimming its circuit

The crew of the **Miss Debb** *unload their great white onto the docks at Phillips Seafood in Crescent, Georgia. (Photo: Debbie Kehle)*

near the Finneys' boat, the great white departed for good and did not return to the location, at least not while the Finneys were still there.

Fortunately, the Finneys were able to take some photos of their visitor. In some of these, several remoras are clearly visible swimming along with the shark. There is also a mass of what appears to be a hunk of flesh just below the surface near the shark. This object, and not the Finneys, was probably what piqued the great white's interest.

The crew of the Miss Debb with their second great white shark. This one was taken roughly 18 miles off the Georgia coast in January 1995. Pictured are Captain Rodney Kehle, Mitchell Tootle and Danny O'Connell. (Photo: Debbie Kehle)

Great whites have been landed all along the Georgia coast. Historically, though, accounts of great whites only go back as far as the late 20th century. When one realizes that the first documented photographic proof of these large sharks' existence in Georgia waters was taken in the 1990's, one realizes just how much there is to learn about great whites off Georgia.

Fossil evidence indicates that white sharks have been swimming in the ocean off Georgia for millions of years, so this naturally raises the question of why are reports of these large sharks of so recent vintage? The answer is unclear, but it has more to do with human perceptions than shark behavior. As with other locales along the southeast coast, sharks were often divided into groups called maneaters, sand sharks or hammerheads. With such cosmopolitan groupings, it is hard to distinguish great whites from bull sharks or tiger sharks whenever maneaters were chronicled in the days of yore.

Since the 1970's, there have been several great whites encountered not far offshore. Prior to the moratorium on landing these large sharks, some were actually caught by fishermen which were brought back to shore and confirmed as great whites. For instance, in 1995, a great white was landed within five miles of Cumberland Island by a commercial fisherman working out of Florida.

Ansley recalls that there have been several white sharks reported to the Georgia Department of Natural Resources down through the years. "There were a couple of small white sharks caught commercially in the eighties and landed, but, again, no photo documentation," he noted. "It was called in by a dealer, but under landings information, sharks are grouped and rarely broken down by species. Another small white reported to us was caught commercially, I believe, in the early 90's. That fish was immediately purchased and supposedly put on a truck for New York before we could get to the docks. I got the coordinates for where the fish was caught—about 60 nautical miles offshore in 25 fathoms. But, again, no picture."

On January 5th, 1994, Captain Rodney Kehle and the crew of the shark fishing boat, *Miss Debb* hauled in a white shark while longlining for shark approximately 18 miles off Jekyll Island. Less than six feet long, this shark was not large enough to impress Kehle and his men, who frequently caught larger sharks than this one in the waters near their home port of Brunswick, Georgia. Their usual haul included sandbar sharks, hammerheads, lemon sharks, and bull sharks. One particularly memorable catch was a tiger shark that weighed 1,100 pounds.

In February 1995, the crew of the **Miss Debb** *caught their third great white shark, this one just three miles off Daytona Beach, Florida. (Photo: Debbie Kehle)*

"There are some really big sharks out there, bigger than most folks would believe," said Kehle. "We've caught lots of 300 to 500 pound sharks that were hooked on the longline, but when we got to them, we found that something had bitten them off clean with one bite right behind the gills. The only sharks in these waters big enough to do that would be a tiger shark or a great white."

What caught the men's attention on this cool winter day was the fact that the shark was of a species that none of them had ever dealt with before. Though it looked similar to a mako, Kehle could tell that he was looking at something different because of the sharp serrated teeth which the shark had in its mouth, unlike a mako whose teeth are smooth. Though not as common as other species, the men of the *Miss Debb* had caught plenty of makos in the past. As a matter of fact, they even landed a 400 pound mako on this very same trip.

"We had caught makos before, so I knew what they looked like," recalled Kehle. "I had never personally seen a white shark before, but I had seen photos of great whites in books and on television, and this looked more like one of them than a mako. We had out eight miles of line with 500 baited hooks attached at regular intervals. When we winched in the gear on board, there were some sandbar sharks hooked for the first couple of miles, but there was a two mile stretch of line with nothing on it, and then we hauled this shark in. When we kept winching in the gear, there was another long stretch with nothing hooked, and after about two miles we got to some more sandbar sharks. That shark had all the line to himself, which was very unusual."

Based on his knowledge and experience with sharks, Kehle was fairly certain that the shark was a great white, but he wanted confirmation of the identity of his catch from someone who was an expert in identifying sharks. During his eight years of fishing for sharks from Cape Lookout to Cape Canaveral, he had never caught a white shark, nor had he ever heard of any other fishermen landing a great white off the Georgia coast. Thus he was a little uncomfortable stating unequivocally that he had indeed caught a great white. Fortunately, thanks to his past interactions with marine biologists and their students who sometimes studied the sharks he caught, Kehle was able to contact several shark specialists who were willing to take a look at his shark.

Shark researchers George Burgess of the International Shark Attack File at the Florida Museum of Natural History and Dr. Franklin Snelson of the University of Central Florida were among the crowd of onlookers on hand when Kehle arrived at the dock at Phillips' Seafood near the small community of Crescent, Georgia. The researchers brought along some students to help examine the shark. When asked about the experience, Snelson told a reporter from the *Florida Times-Union*, "I've been in this business 30 years and this is the first one I've seen." For Burgess, this was only the second great white that the noted ichthyologist had observed in the field. He was on hand when another juvenile great white was landed twenty years earlier off Cape Lookout in North Carolina.

After thoroughly studying the sharks, researchers determined that it was a juvenile male great white, approximately two weeks old. The shark had a total length of 5 feet 4 inches, and weighed 163 pounds.

The photos of this shark are the earliest known photographic evidence that shows a great white caught in Georgia waters. There may be other photos lurking about in family albums or tucked away deep in the archives that depict a great white shark caught previous to 1994, but so far none have come to light.

Great whites are so infrequently caught in these waters that the chance of an individual actually landing one is extremely remote. When asked about the likelihood of catching another white shark, Kehle told a reporter from the local newspaper, "I doubt if I'll ever see one again. But you never know." Ironically, just over a year later and near the exact same spot, the Georgia shark fisherman landed his second great white.

This particular shark was caught in January of 1995, as the *Miss*

Debb was fishing in the same waters that produced the white shark the previous year. This shark, which was over 10 feet long and weighed 593 pounds, was much bigger than Kehle's first great white. The shark was hauled aboard and taken back to Brunswick. Despite being larger in size, this shark did not generate the interest of his earlier shark, and there were no groups of inquisitive scientists or reporters from the local newspapers on hand to investigate the fish.

Kehle landed yet another white shark a month later after shifting his operations south to fish for sharks off the Florida coast between Cape Canaveral and Jacksonville. This was the third great white he landed in just over a year's time, and the second in a month.

"We caught this shark three miles off the beach there at Daytona," recalled Kehle. "We caught a lot of sharks in those waters, especially in the waters off Canaveral. This was because there were a lot of scallopers working those waters that time of year, and the sharks followed these boats. The water temperature was between 62° and 68°, and the shark was caught in 40 feet of water. This great white was over 10 feet long, and weighed 586 pounds."

These reports of encounters with great whites off the coast of Georgia demonstrate that not only are these rare sharks present in these waters, but they are more prevalent than one might think. Several questions need to be answered before we can begin to understand the relationship of these apex predators with the marine ecosystem off the Georgia coast. Do they live here all year off the edge of the continental shelf, or are they just passing through? Right now, no one really knows.

8
GREAT WHITE SHARK ATTACKS OFF THE CAROLINA & GEORGIA COASTS

"Having seized me it went tearing through the water. I could feel it bound forward at each stroke of its tail. Had it not been for my copper helmet my head would have been torn off by the rush through the water. I was perfectly conscious, but somehow I felt no terror at all. There was only a feeling of numbness. I wondered how long it would be before those teeth would crunch through, and whether they would strike first into my back or my breast."
—from an account of a Spanish diver who was attacked by a great white shark in Beaufort Inlet.

T he Beaufort Bar is an underwater sand bank where the waters of Beaufort Inlet meet the Atlantic Ocean. This place has a special spot in pirate lore, and is recognized by historians and pirate enthusiasts the world over as the place where Blackbeard lost his flagship, the *Queen Anne's Revenge*. Researchers and divers have explored this sandy place looking for evidence which proves that the remains of an old ship found in the sand here belonged to the wily old pirate.

But back in the 1880's, it was the story of the misadventures of a Spanish diver which focused worldwide attention on the waters between Bogue Banks and Shackleford Banks. In September of 1883, a sailing vessel known as the *Atlanta* went down in a storm on the inlet side of Beaufort Bar. The ship's owners, hoping to save whatever they could of their valuable ship and its cargo, engaged the services of a professional diving crew to bring what they could back to the surface.

We do not know the name of the company they hired, the vessel they used, nor any of the names of the crew except for the aforementioned Spanish diver named Alfetto. We would not even know his name were it not for an encounter with a great white shark that nearly turned fatal.

One day in January of 1884, Alfetto and another diver were on the bottom of the sea hard at work on the remains of the *Atlanta*. After a few successful dives, the men decided to return to the surface. The Spaniard sent his companion up first, and planned to follow him up to the surface and rest once they had taken the piece of wreckage they were then working with to their boat. As the unnamed diver was being hauled through the water to the surface, he watched in horror as a large great white shark grabbed his diving partner, carrying the poor man away in its mouth. When he finally made his way back into the boat, the diver frantically related to his shipmates what he had seen befall the Spaniard in the watery depths below. As the man finished with his story, those onboard were sure that their companion would be killed and eaten by the ravenous shark. But just as they were ready to give up on their friend, Alfetto surfaced approximately fifty yards from their boat.

He was unconscious when they reached him, but fortunately still alive. He bore no wounds on his body, but his metal diving suit bore the scars of the encounter as there were several holes left behind by the shark's razor-sharp teeth. They could only guess as to why the large shark had attacked their friend in the first place, but what was even more puzzling was why the shark had let him go. Perhaps he did not like the taste of the copper diving suit.

Alfetto slowly recovered, and after more than a day of recuperating from his ordeal, he was finally able to speak with his companions and tell them what had happened on the bottom of the sea at Beaufort Inlet. Here is Alfetto's amazing first-person account of his terrifying encounter in the waters just off Fort Macon.

"As you know, we had made our fourth descent, and, while my companion clambered into the vessel, I waited on the ground till he should attach the cords to draw something out. I was just about to signal to be drawn up for a moment's rest when I noticed a shadowy body moving at some distance above me and towards me. In a moment every fish had disappeared, the very crustacean lay still upon the sand, and the cuttle-fish scurried away as fast as they could. I was not thinking of danger, and my first thought was that it was the shadow of a passing boat. But suddenly a feeling of terror seized me; I felt impelled to flee from something; I knew not what; a vague horror seemed grasping after me such as a child fancies when leaving a darkened room. By this time the shadow had come nearer and taken shape. It scarcely needed a glance to show me that it was a man-eater, and of the largest size. Had I signaled to be drawn up then it would have been certain death. All I could do was to remain still until it left. It lay off twenty-five feet, just outside the rigging of the ship, its body motionless, its fins barely stirring the water about its gills. It was a monster as it was, but to add to the horror the pressure of the water upon my head made it appear as if pouring flames from its eyes and mouth, and every movement of its fins and tail seemed accompanied by a display of fireworks. I was sure the fish was thirty feet long, and so near that I could see its double row of white teeth. Involuntarily I shrank closer to the side of the vessel. But the first movement betrayed my presence. I saw the shining eyes fixed upon me; its tail quivered, as it darted at me like a streak of light. I shrank closer to the side of the ship. I saw it turn on its side, its mouth open, and heard the teeth snap as it darted by me. It had missed me, but only for a moment. The sweep of its mighty tail had thrown me forward. I saw it turn, balance itself, and its tail quivered as it darted by me again. There was no escape. It turned on its back as it swooped down on me like a hawk on a sparrow. The cavernous jaws opened, and the long shining teeth grated as they closed on my metal harness. It had me. I could feel its teeth grinding upon my copper breastplate as it tried to bite me in two; for fortunately it had caught me just across the middle, where I was best protected. Having seized me it went tearing through the water. I could feel it bound forward at each stroke of its tail. Had it not been for my copper helmet my head would have been torn off by the rush through the water. I was perfectly conscious, but somehow I felt no terror at all. There was only a feeling of numbness. I wondered how long it would be before those teeth would crunch through, and whether they would strike first into my back or my breast. Then I thought of Maggie and the baby, and wondered who would take care of them, and if she would ever know what had become of me. All these thoughts had passed through my brain in an instant, but in that time the connecting air tube had been snapped, and my head seemed ready to burst with pressure when the monster's teeth kept crunching and grinding away upon my harness. Then I felt the cold water begin to pour in and heard the bubble, bubble, bubble, as the air escaped into the creature's mouth. I began to hear great guns, and to see fireworks and rainbows and sunshine, and all kinds of pretty things; then I thought I was floating away on a rosy summer cloud, dreaming to the sound of sweet music. Then all became blank. The shark might have eaten me then at his leisure, and I never would have been the wiser. Imagine my astonishment, then, when I opened my eyes on board this boat and saw you fellows around me. Yes, sir! I thought I was dead and eaten up, sure."

There is no denying the fact that great whites occasionally attack humans. According to the International Shark Attack File, in the 420 years from 1580 to 2000, these sharks were responsible for 254 unprovoked attacks on people throughout the world. The chances of being attacked by any species of shark in the waters off the east coast of the United States from Cape Hatteras to the Georgia coast are rather small. The chances of a person being the victim of a great white shark attack along this same stretch of coast are even more remote.

"They're a cold water form," noted Dr. Schwartz. "There are so few that are near shore that the possibility of their attacking is almost nil."

Although rare, white shark attacks have occurred in these waters, often with catastrophic consequences. According to the ISAF, there have been seven *officially* recorded unprovoked shark attacks on humans attributed to the handiwork of great whites in the United States along the Atlantic Ocean and Gulf of Mexico. Only two of the attacks listed in the ISAF's files occurred south of Chesapeake Bay, one from North Carolina and one from South Carolina. None were reported from Georgia waters.

There are several encounters with white sharks that have not made their way into the ISAF's database, which is a work in progress that continues to accumulate accounts of shark attacks from around the world. Their records only mention the two white shark attacks from the middle of the twentieth century. Yet there are earlier attacks, such as Alfetto's misadventure from 1884.

The earliest shark attack chronicled in the waters of the southeastern United States that may have been the handiwork of a great white is the incident surrounding the two massive sharks off Charleston mentioned earlier. Recalling an incident that occurred fifty years in the past, Captain William Ferguson described two huge sharks implicated in separate fatal human encounters. He described both incidents to a reporter from the *Charleston News and Courier*. Since the incidents are quite remarkable, they are included here.

"In Charleston Harbor, about 1840, as near as I can recall, one of the crew of a pilot boat was accidentally thrown overboard. The boat was lowering her sails and coming up to her wharf at the time. The two men pulling a skiff to his rescue were passed by a large shark, which took the man under, and he was never seen again. The morning paper noted that the man was treading water lightly with his chest out. The shark was said to be twenty-five feet long.

"A large shark caught with hook and line on Southern wharf had in it a part of a white man's body with a portion of his sailor's clothes about it. This, too, was said to be a twenty-five foot shark. The date of this, as near as I can remember, was 1837."

As stated earlier, there is no way of knowing for certain which species of shark was described by Captain Ferguson. His memory of events fifty years earlier may have led to some inaccuracies or exaggerations, especially regarding the shark's enormous proportions. Then again, he may have been spot on with his recollection of the events, in which case it is almost certain that the guilty sharks were great whites, the only species of sharks in these waters that could possibly reach 25 feet in length and consume large mammals. But until we get a more definitive description of the shark, Captain Ferguson's tale will have to remain in the realm of good sea lore.

One of the more enigmatic shark attacks along the North Carolina coast which may have been the work of a great white shark happened off the Outer Banks of North Carolina during the waning days of World War II. Information on this incident is hard to come by due to a number of factors, including wartime censorship still in place at the time the attack took place, and the secret nature of the activities of the military unit to which the victim was assigned.

What we do know is that this attack occurred in the surf along the beach near where the airport now stands on Ocracoke Island. On August 16th, 1945, several men from the Beach Jumper Units who were training at the Amphibious Training Base Ocracoke were relaxing as the enlisted men had been given a field day on the beach to celebrate news of the surrender of Japan. One of these men was John Edward Kuenstier, a man about whom little information has been recorded. His grave marker at the National Cemetery in New Bern mentions that the 22 year old sailor held the rank of EM3C, and was assigned to BJU-7. This was Beach Jumper

Unit 7, which was part of a unit of commandos and special operations personnel which had their headquarters at ATB Ocracoke.

Details about what happened that day are sketchy, and naval records give scant information about the incident. But C. Felix Harvey of Kinston, who was one of the naval officers present at the outing, was an eyewitness to the vicious attack and remembers the event quite vividly. As it was getting later in the afternoon, Kuenstier decided to take a swim. "He swam out past the breakers a good ways, about fifty or so yards off the beach," recalled Harvey. "Next thing we knew, we heard him yelling and screaming. At first we thought he was having a heart attack or something. But then we saw a trail of blood on the water, and knew it was a shark. We managed to get him back to the beach, but he died right there before the ambulance could take him to the infirmary. The shark had bitten him twice. The first time it hit him on the lower part of his leg, but you could see where its teeth had been stopped and deflected by the bone. Then it took another bite, this one in the large muscle of the thigh. The bite mark was 13 inches wide, and it nearly took his leg off."

Afterwards, Harvey was instructed by Captain Anthony Rorschach to compile a report about the incident, as well as any other similar encounters with sharks in the area. Unfortunately, the report he prepared and submitted to his captain has been lost down through the years. But Harvey recalls that his interviews with several of the local residents turned up some interesting information.

"I spoke with several of the older folks and they told me this was not the first time a shark had killed somebody at Ocracoke. I documented two cases in particular that stood out to me, one from 1900, and another from 1905. In both cases, the victims were drum fishermen who were wearing waders as they fished in the water there at the tip of Ocracoke where it meets Ocracoke Inlet. "

As stated earlier, there has been much speculation as to the identity of the shark that killed Kuenstier. There is a persistent rumor that this was the handiwork of a great white shark. Harvey remembers some traits about the shark, but never specified which exact species had done the deed.

"We felt at the time that we actually caught the shark that was responsible for this attack just a short time afterwards. We fished that area pretty good, and one of us brought in a shark that was ten feet long, and when we measured its mouth, it was the same size as the bite in the sailor's leg, which was 13 inches wide. So several of us were satisfied that we had caught the shark. We didn't know exactly which species in particular it was. Could have been a great white, I don't know for sure. But I do know that it wasn't a hammerhead."

Was this attack the handiwork of a great white? This question is still open to debate. There were several people along the Outer Banks who thought it was, and worked hard to make sure word of the incident did not spread too far. Hopefully Harvey's original report and photos of Kuenstier's wounds will turn up in the future and shed more light on this shark attack.

The best documented twentieth century incident in which a great white was blamed for a fatal unprovoked shark attack in Carolina waters occurred on July 15th, 1957, in the waters off Atlantic Beach in Carteret County, not far from where Alfetto had his memorable adventure with a great white back in 1884. Unfortunately, the victim on this occasion, Rupert Wade, did not survive the ordeal.

A 57-year-old resident of Morehead City, Wade was a renowned long distance swimmer who often amazed the tourists at the local beaches with his swimming stamina. On this particular occasion, he was over a thousand feet offshore swimming with a lifeguard named Billy Shaw. After about 15 minutes in the water, Wade yelled out to his companion that a shark had bitten him. He told Shaw to swim for shore and get help, which his friend promptly did.

The Coast Guard was immediately summoned from Fort Macon. When they arrived, Coast Guard crewmen spotted Wade floating on the water. Alive but unconscious, he was lifted into the boat and taken to the Coast Guard station where an ambulance was waiting. Despite the fact that they administered artificial respiration on the trip back, they were unable to revive Wade, who was pronounced dead at the Morehead City hospital. He bled to death as a result of the wounds inflicted by the shark.

The death of Wade was attributed to the work of a great white shark. He was bitten on the right leg midway between his hip and knee, ripping deep enough into his flesh to expose the bone in his leg. He also had several deep cuts on his right foot.

Four years after the incident at Atlantic Beach, another shark attack in the Carolinas was attributed to a great white. On August 16th, 1961, a 19 year old student named William Lee Bailey was swimming in approximately six feet of water off Pawley's Island, South Carolina, when he was attacked by what an eyewitness described as a great white. The shark took off the young man's leg, and severely injured his arm. Fortunately, first aid was rendered in time to stop him from bleeding to death.

According to the International Shark Attack File, Bailey's misadventure is the only confirmed great white shark attack on a human to occur in the waters of South Carolina. But there was at least one other report of a great white shark attack in the Palmetto State. In this instance the victim was a boat.   On the evening of September 26th, 1959, two Marine Corps officers from the nearby Marine base decided to head out for some fishing in their off-duty hours. Captain E.J. Hines, Major W. Waller and his son, Larry, went fishing in the waters of Albergotti Creek near Beaufort, South Carolina. Just before midnight, their 12-foot boat was attacked by what they described as, "a man-eating white shark."

Despite their best efforts to elude the unwelcome visitor, the shark was persistent, and continued tracking the boat and ramming it. After two and a half hours, they finally lost the great white in shallow water. Fortunately, none of the group was injured.

For many years, experts have tried to figure out exactly why sharks attack humans. There are some fascinating theories bandied about, but in the end there is still no simple answer to this question. There are many precautions a person can take to minimize the risk of being the victim of a shark attack, but researchers have much to learn in this field of study in order to fully understand why sharks, including great whites, sometimes attack humans, even here along the Carolina coast.

9
WHITE $HARK CONSERVATION

In October of 2004, great white sharks obtained worldwide protection thanks to actions taken in Bangkok, Thailand, by delegates to the 13th Convention on International Trade of Endangered Species (CITES) summit. Australia and Madagascar made the joint proposal in an effort to protect these sharks, whose numbers are believed by many to be dwindling around the world, and are facing the danger of being hunted to extinction.

Those who supported the measure point out that great white sharks are under increasing threats worldwide mainly due to excessive and unregulated trade. Australian delegates argued that great whites were the target of, "a huge unsustainable trade," especially in sharks' teeth and jaws, which are worth thousands of dollars to collectors. Others are killed in the notorious shark fin industry which supplies Asia with shark fins for soup.

Ian Creswell, head of the Australian delegation, was happy that the countries of the world had taken action to protect great whites. "Australia is very pleased that the parties to CITES have recognized the importance of regulating trade in great white sharks in order to promote their conservation." Australian officials estimate that there are less than 10,000 great whites swimming in the waters off the Land Down Under. They point out that records of these sharks in the waters of South Australia have dropped by 94% since the 1980's.

The decline is not unique to Australia. Scientists from Dalhousie University in Halifax, Nova Scotia, studied data compiled by pelagic longline swordfish and tuna fishing fleets in the northwestern part of the Atlantic Ocean to try to determine the abundance of sharks in the area. Their research, conducted over a 15 year period between 1986 and 2001, showed an alarming decline in numbers of several larger shark species, including great whites. "Using the largest data set in the Northwest Atlantic, we show rapid large declines in large coastal and oceanic shark populations," they wrote. "Scallopped hammerhead, white and thresher sharks are each estimated to have declined by over 75% in the past 15 years."

Not everyone agrees with these bleak forecasts, and there are many who believe such dire predictions of the eminent destruction of the large sharks are based on faulty data. There are many shark fishermen whose lives have been adversely affected by government efforts to regulate the shark fishing industry. Some have gone out of business, while others have merely moved to places where shark fishing and the money it generates are welcomed. Many view sharks as a renewable natural resource, and though it should be managed wisely, a ban on catching large sharks such as great whites is unnecessary and unreasonable.

White sharks will be slow in recovering from any exploitation because they are not very prolific. The female is believed to reach sexual maturity at fifteen years old, and has a relatively small number of offspring. Gestation is thought to take approximately a year, so any given female would only produce offspring biennially. With such a slow rate of reproduction, it will take years for the population of great whites to recover from any stresses placed upon it from overfishing.

The greatest obstacle facing those who would save these apex predators is lack of knowledge. Our study of the world's oceans and the creatures that dwell therein is in its infancy. In the past hundred years, mankind has just begun to explore the part of the planet that lies beneath the surface of the seas. As our knowledge of the oceans becomes more complete, we may find that white sharks are alive in numbers we can hardly imagine. But until that time, it is important to take measures to preserve these large predators so future generations can learn more about these remarkable creatures, and their place in the world.

BIBLIOGRAPHY

• Allen, Thomas B., *Shadows In the Sea*, The Lyons Press, 1996.

• Baun, Julie, et. al., "Collapse and Conservation of Shark Populations in the Northwest Atlantic," *Science*, Vol. 299, pp. 381-392, 17 January 2003.

• Beardon, Charles, *Elasmobranch Fishes of South Carolina*, Bear Bluff Laboratories, 1965.

• Bjorndal, Karen A., ed., *Biology and Conservation of Sea Turtles*, Revised Edition, Smithsonian Institution, 1995.

• Braswell, Tommy, "Angler gets 'great white' Christmas surprise," *Charleston Post and Courier*, 31 December 1995.

• Bright, Michael, *The Private Life of Sharks*, Stackpole Books, 2000.

• Brown, Aycock, "Maneaters Rare off Coast," *News and Observer*, 28 May 1930.

• Burton, E. Milby, "Shark Attacks along the South Carolina Coast," *Scientific Monthly*, March, 1935.

• Casey, John G., and Harold L. Pratt, "Distribution of the White Shark, *Carcharodon carcharias*, in the Western North Atlantic," *Memoirs of the Southern California Academy of Sciences*, 9, pp. 2-14. 1985.

• Castro, Jose, *The Sharks of North American Waters*. Texas A&M Press, 1983.

• Cheek, Larry, "A Scare at the Beach," *Fayetteville Observer*, 14 June 1989.

• Clancy, Paul, "Great Whites: Two of the Fearsome Predators Caught Off Virginia Coast," *Norfolk Virginian-Pilot*, 14 November 2000.

• Coles, Russell J., —"Notes on the Sharks and Rays of Cape Lookout, N.C." *Proceedings of the Biological Society of Washington*, April 13, 1915.

– "The Large Sharks of Cape Lookout, North Carolina. The White Shark or Maneater, Tiger Shark and Hammerhead," *Copeia*, 69:34-43, 1919.

• Ellis, R., and J.E. McCosker, *Great White Shark.* Stanford University Press, 1991.

• Gilbert, Perry, "Fishing at Cojimar," *Sea Frontiers*, Volume 7, Number 1, February 1961.

• Gregg, William H., *Where, When and How to Catch Fish on the East Coast of Florida*, The Matthews-Northrup Works, 1902.

• Halton, Beau, "No Reason To Have Great White Fears," *Florida Times-Union*, 6 January 1997.

• Klimley, A. Peter, *The Secret Life of Sharks*, Simon & Schuster, 2003.

—and David G. Ainley, editors, *Great White Sharks The Biology of Carcharodon Carcharias*, Academic Press, 1996.

• Larson, Lewis, *Aboriginal Subsistence Technology on the Southeastern Coastal Plain During the Late Prehistoric Period*, University Presses of Florida, 1980.

• "A Monster Shark," *The Weekly Record*, Beaufort, N.C., 18 May 1888.

• Moore, Joseph Curtis, "Distribution of Marine Mammals to Florida Waters," *The American Midland Naturalist*, 49 (1), 1953.

• Nelson, D.R., "Silent Savages," *Oceans* 1:8-22, 1969.

• Radcliffe, Lewis, "The Sharks and Rays of Beaufort, North Carolina," *Bulletin of the U.S. Bureau of Fisheries*, 34: 239-384, 1914.

• Randall, John E., "Size of the Great White Shark (Carcharodon),"
Science, Volume 181, July 12, 1973.

• Robertson, Pat, "Great White Caught Off SC Coast Not So Great,"
The State, 11 July 1993.

• Robins, C. Richard, et. al., *Common and Scientific Names of Fishes
from the United States and Canada*, 5th Edition, American Fisheries Society,
1991.

• Schwartz, Frank J., *Sharks of the Carolinas*, NCDNER, 1989.

—*Sharks, Skates and Rays of the Carolinas.* UNC Press, 2003.

—and George Burgess, *Sharks of North Carolina and Adjacent
Waters*, NCDNER, 1975.

• Schwartz, Mark, "Great white sharks migrate thousands of miles
across the sea, new study finds," *Stanford Report*, 2 January 2002.

• "Shark Expert Confirms Great White Off St. Augustine," *First Coast
News*, 10 June 2005.

• "Shark Makes Try to Overturn Boat of Marine Giggers," *Beaufort
Gazette*, 8 October 1959.

• Smith, Hugh, *The Fishes of North Carolina*, Bulletin of the N.C.
Geological & Economic Survey, 1907.

• Springer, Stewart, "Note on the Sharks of Florida," *Proceedings of
the Florida Academy of Sciences*, Volume 3, 1938.

— "The great white shark, Carcharodon carcharias (Linnaeus), in
Florida water," *Copeia*, 1939:114-115.

—"Field Observations on Large Sharks of the Florida-Caribbean
Region." in *Sharks and Survival*, Perry Gilbert, ed., D. Heath & Co., 1963.

— "It Began With a Shark," in *Dissertations on Steno as Geologist*, edited by Gustav Scherz, Odense Un. Press, 1971.

• Stringer, Rick, "Observations of Inshore South Carolina Sharks 1967 to 2000," unpublished manuscript, 2004.

• Travis, William, *Shark for Sale*, Rand McNally & Company, 1961.

• Tricas, Timothy and John E. McCosker, "Predatory Behavior of the White Shark (Carcharodon carcharias) With Notes On Its Biology," *Proceedings of the California Academy of Sciences*, Vol. 43, No., 14, pp. 221-238. July 12, 1984.

INDEX